MW00489336

IMMEASURABLY
More!

AN IN-DEPTH STUDY
OF EPHESIANS

ELIZABETH BAGWELL
FICKEN

Immeasurably More! © Copyright 2004, 2016 by Elizabeth Bagwell Ficken
Printed in the United States of America
First Printing, 2004
W & E Publishing, Cary, NC

Unless otherwise noted, Scripture quotations are from the Holy Bible,
New King James Version, copyright © 1979, 1980, 1982, Thomas Nelson,
Inc. Publishers. Used by permission. All rights reserved.

Scripture quotations identified NASB are from the
New American Standard Bible © The Lockman Foundation, 1960, 1962,
1963, 1968, 1971, 1972, 1973, 1975, 1977. Used by permission.

Scripture quotations identified NIV are from the *New International Version*,
copyright © 1973, 1978, 1984 by International Bible Society.

Scripture quotations identified NLT are from the Holy Bible,
New Living Translation, copyright © 1996. Used by permission of
Tyndale House Publisher, Inc., Wheaton, Illionois 60189. All rights reserved.

Scripture quotations identified The Message are from *THE MESSAGE*.
Copyright © by Eugene H. Peterson, 1993, 1994, 1995.
Used by permission of NavPress Publishing Group.

Scripture quotations identified KJV are from the *King James Version*.

"Do you know Jesus?" Gospel presentation from Sonlife Classic.
Copyright © 2009 Used by permission.

Cover: Jeannine Klingbeil

Special thanks to:
Kathy Peterson, who has journeyed with me through the seasons of life
and who has discussed with me everything we can think of about life in Christ;
Kathleen Harwood, whose questions and thoughts prompted me to write an in-depth
women's Bible study; and my mother, Susan Bagwell, for reading my school papers,
correcting my grammar, and always showing me the unconditional love of the Lord.

Now to Him who is able to do immeasurably more than all we ask or imagine,
according to His power that is at work within us, to Him be glory in the church
and in Christ Jesus throughout all generations, for ever and ever! Amen.
Ephesians 3:20-21 ^{NIV}

ISBN-10: 0-9905933-1-2
ISBN-13: 978-0-9905933-1-7

TABLE OF CONTENTS

INTRODUCTION

Dear Friend,

You are about to encounter the amazing truths of being in Christ. In Ephesians, you will find that you have been blessed with every spiritual blessing, that you have an inheritance of indefinable worth, and that God's great power that raised Christ from the dead is available to you! That's just Chapter 1!

This book of the Bible is so very precious to me. It's my favorite. I love the beautiful, extravagant language of Paul as he describes the absolutely amazing and unending grace and love of the Lord. I love the deep, overwhelming concepts of the gospel and the clear, practical explanations of how to walk worthy of the Lord. I love the way this letter lays out the doctrine that we are to believe and then spells out the details of how we are to behave.

Every time that I read Ephesians, I am either encouraged, challenged, inspired, convicted, or delighted. No matter where you are in your spiritual journey, the truths of what God did in Christ for us will be meaningful to you.

There is immeasurably more to discover in this rich letter to the church in Ephesus. May the Lord open the eyes of your understanding, may the Lord show you what He has done for you, and may the Lord mold you more closely to the image of Christ as you hear from Him in His word.

I hope that you will find this study of Ephesians exciting and encouraging. It will be a lot of work, but the truths of God's Word are worth every single moment of time and ounce of effort we expend.

Now to Him who is able to do immeasurably more than all we can ask or imagine, according to His power that is at work within us, to Him be glory in the church and in Christ Jesus throughout all generations, for ever and ever! Amen!

MY BIBLE STORY

I love my Bible! But I have about 10 of them on my bookshelf, so which one do I love and use to read and study? I'd like to answer that question with my Bible story.

The earliest Bible that I remember reading was a children's New Testament Living Bible. It was a birthday present from a friend when I was eight years old! I tried to read the book of Revelation, but didn't get very far. The next special Bible that I received was a black (faux) leather King James Version with Susan Elizabeth Bagwell engraved in gold letters on the front. This was from my parents, and it was my church Bible. I don't remember reading it at all, but I must have taken it to Sunday School with me because I found a Psalm 23 bookmark in it. That was to become the first well-known Scripture to me.

When I was fourteen I began using a paperback Bible which my father felt was an excellent translation. The New English Bible is not very well known, but it was the Bible that helped me begin to know God's Word. My Sunday school teacher actually made us read and study Ephesians so I began taking this Bible to church. I also underlined verses and took it with me to Bible studies in high school.

My first Bible with cross-references and helpful notes was the Ryrie Study Bible in the King James Version. A friend took me to the Baptist Bookstore, and I experienced picking out a Bible for myself. It was bound in dark blue leather and Elizabeth Bagwell was engraved in silver lettering. I bought it after high school graduation and used it for my quiet times and Bible study and sermon notes for about 10 years—through college and early marriage and the births of my children! It was falling apart and the bookbinder recommended a durable covering: blue canvas. I call it my blue jean Bible now!

Then I became aware of the New King James Version and decided it would be nice to leave behind the Thee's and Thou's of the Old King James . . . so I bought The Woman's Study Bible NJKV. It was refreshing to read God's truths in a new translation in a Bible that had clean pages where I could make new notes. Familiar verses were lovely and overlooked verses began to stand out as they had not done before. The changing of Bible translations became a new adventure for me.

I own and have read through the Bible in the NIV, NLT, NET, NAS, NKJ, ESV, and I'm currently reading through the HCSB. It is important to me to have a Bible with helpful study notes: historical and cultural information; word study definitions; maps; and appropriate cross-references. The layout of the Scriptures on the pages is important too! It just has to feel right! I have used the Archeological Study Bible and the Life Application Bible, but have enjoyed the Nelson Study Bible and the Holman Christian Standard Study Bible more.

Jesus loves me this I know, for my Bible tells me so! I love God's Word and I love my Bible—whichever one I may be reading at any given time.

Do You Know Jesus?

This is the most important question in this study. Please notice that I didn't ask you if you know about Jesus. But do you know Him, personally?

The Bible teaches that God loves you.
"For God so loved the world . . . that He gave His one and only son that whoever believes in Him will not perish, but have eternal life." John 3:16 ᴱˢⱽ

And it teaches that God wants you to know Him personally.
"Now this is eternal life, that men may know Him, the only true God, and Jesus Christ whom He has sent." John 17:3 ᴱˢⱽ

But . . . people are separated from God by their sin.
"Your sinful acts have alienated you from your God" Isaiah 59:2 ᴺᴱᵀ

Sin causes us to miss the very best for our life.
"Jesus said, 'I came that you might have life and have it to the full." John 10:10 ᴺᴵⱽ

Sin causes us to face death and judgment.
"The wages of sin is death." Romans 3:32 ᴺᴬˢ
"Those who do not know God . . . will pay the penalty of eternal destruction away from the presence of the Lord." 2 Thessalonians 1:8-9 ᴺᴬˢ

But there is a solution! Jesus Christ died and conquered death for you! We deserve death and judgment, but Jesus took upon Himself the punishment for our sins, so that we could have a personal relationship with God.
"For there is only one God and one Mediator who can reconcile God and humanity-- the man Christ Jesus. He gave his life to purchase freedom for everyone." 1 Timothy 2:5-6 ᴺᴸᵀ

It's not enough just to know this. Each of us by faith must receive Jesus Christ if we want to know God personally.
"To all who have received Him—those who believe in His name—He has given the right to become God's children." John 1:12 ᴺᴱᵀ
"For it is by grace you have been saved, through faith—and this not from yourselves, it is the gift of God." Ephesians 2:8 ᴺᴵⱽ

The ABC's of faith involve:
<u>Acknowledging your need</u>—admitting you have sinned and desiring to turn from sin. (1 John 1:8-9)
<u>Believing Jesus Christ died in your place</u> and rose again to be your Savior—providing forgiveness for your sins. (1 Corinthians 15:3-4:17)
<u>Choosing to invite Christ</u> to direct your life. (Romans 10:9)

Your desire to have a personal relationship with God can be expressed through a simple prayer like this:
"Dear Lord, I want to know You personally. Thank you for sending Jesus who died in my place and rose again to be my Savior. Please forgive my sins. I am willing, with your help, to turn from my sins. Come into my life and lead me. Amen."

*For illustrations and more information, go to **KnowHimPersonally.com***

ℋ E L P F U L ℋ I N T S

If you are new to in-depth Bible study. You will need a Bible. Please feel free to use the version of your choice. There are many translations. If you are using a Catholic Bible or a Jewish Old Testament it will be helpful for you to also use a modern version of the Bible which includes the Old and New Testament.

I recommend the following versions which are available for free at online Bible study websites, in smartphone and tablet apps (see recommendations on the next page), or for purchase in Christian bookstores. They are usually referred to by the letters in parentheses.

New King James Version (NKJV)   New American Standard Version (NASB)
New International Version (NIV)   Holman Christian Standard Bible (HCSB)
English Standard Version (ESV)

This study was written using multiple translations. I have found that I can gain understanding of the meaning of verses by reading other versions of the same passage. Two other popular Bibles are *The Message* and the New Living Translation (NLT); these are both wonderful versions for comparative reading, but are not as appropriate for in-depth study.

Planning time for your lesson. Set aside a specific amount of time to work on the lesson. One lesson may take 30-40 minutes depending on your familiarity with the Scriptures. You may want to do the lessons in shorter increments of time, depending on your schedule and personal preferences. I find that I absorb, retain, and apply the message of the Scriptures better when I am not rushed.

Please begin your study time with prayer. Ask the Holy Spirit to give you understanding of God's Word, as it is promised that He will do according to 1 Corinthians 2:12-13: "Now we have received, not the spirit of the world, but the Spirit who is from God, that we might know the things freely given to us by God, which things we also speak, not in words taught by human wisdom, but in those taught by the Spirit, combining spiritual thoughts with spiritual words." I have given you a reminder at the beginning of each lesson.

Observation, interpretation, and application. The Scripture readings, activities, cross-references and word definitions are all placed in the order which is most appropriate to your study. It is best to follow this order if you can, rather than skipping steps or setting steps aside to be completed at a different time. The order follows the inductive study process: observation (what the Scripture says), interpretation (what the author intended, what the Scripture means) and application (what difference the Scripture makes in your life). You will be doing the research, cross-referencing and summarization of the truths of each passage. When you finish a study of a passage, you will have gleaned more understanding on your own than you will find in some commentaries!

Looking up Greek word definitions. One of the activities included to help you understand the correct interpretation of the scripture is discovering and considering the definition of a word in its original language. Please make sure that you look up the definition of the word in its original language, not the definition of the English word. You will be given a prompt like this:

Faith: Strong's #4102
Greek word:
Greek definition:

There are several ways you can look up the words given.

- You can google the Strong's reference number (Strong's 4102) and your web browser will give you links to the definition.
- You can go to an online Bible study website (recommendations below) and use their free reference materials. Look for "study" tabs, "lexicons" (this is what Hebrew and Greek word dictionaries are called), "concordances" and "original language" tools. There are search boxes where you can type in the Strong's reference number. Use G before the number for Greek words (G4102).

studylight.org   blueletterbible.com   searchgodsword.org

Suggested resources, described on page 178, are also available at these websites if you want to do more research on your own.

- You can download free Bible study apps for your smartphone and/or tablet. I use **MySword** which allows me to go to a passage and click on the Strong's reference number next to the word. Try a few different ones and see what you like best.
- You may have some great resources on your own bookshelves! Enjoy using books like: *Strong's Exhaustive Concordance* and *The Complete Word Study Dictionary* by Spiros Zhodiates.

If you have trouble, it would be better to skip the exercise rather than filling in the English definition.

It's about your head and your heart. My hope is that you will read portions of Scripture and gain understanding of what is being communicated through them so that you can consider how to apply the truth of God's Word to your life. I have tried to make the study "user-friendly" and I promise that I don't ask trick questions. I do want to make you think hard sometimes though! I hope you won't get overwhelmed. Do what you can, a little bit at a time. The reward of knowing our holy God through His recorded word far outweighs the time and effort of study.

Prayer requests and praises. You will find pages at the end of this workbook which provide prompts from Scriptures for your prayers as well as a place for you to write out a personal prayer request . If you are studying with a group, it would be helpful to reflect on your personal prayer request before sharing it with the group. Keep your requests brief and personal. This page is also a place to record the prayer requests of others.

UNIT ONE
FROM SINNERS TO SAINTS

LESSON ONE
A TREASURE CHEST OF RICHES
EPHESIANS 1:1 — 6:24

LESSON TWO
TRAVELING TO ANCIENT EPHESUS
ACTS 18 — 20

LESSON THREE
CHANGED LIVES
EPHESIANS 1:1 — 12

LESSON FOUR
SO BLESSED
EPHESIANS 1:3

LESSON ONE
A TREASURE CHEST OF RICHES
EPHESIANS 1:1 — 6:24

> Where your pleasure is, there is your treasure. Where your treasure is, there is your heart. Where your heart is, there is your happiness.[1]
>
> SAINT AUGUSTINE OF HIPPO (354–430)

A treasure hunt! Many children and adults alike enjoy an exciting search with a promised reward at the end of it. The infamous X is usually the main clue on a map showing the location of the prize. But what if you were to receive only a small, torn-off piece of the map? How would you begin? It would be quite difficult, don't you think?

But with the entire map in your possession, you would be able to begin your search with the benefit of many more clues to the treasure. As you begin your study, think of today's exercise as your first look at the whole treasure map. You'll get your bearings, become aware of significant landmarks and gain a basic idea of the layout of the land.

Today, we will look at the whole letter to see the complete context of the treasured truths found in Ephesians. In the first two days of our study, we will read Ephesians 1:1—6:24. We'll look at Paul's reasons for writing, learn something about Paul's circumstances when he wrote the letter and learn a few things about the Ephesians themselves.

Are you ready to discover the riches in Ephesians? Let the exploration begin!

At the beginning of each section, I'll give you a reminder to begin your study time with prayer...remember to depend on the Holy Spirit to teach you the depths of God's Word. Just express your desire to understand and obey the Lord.

Begin your overview of Ephesians by reading the entire book in one sitting. While reading, make notes on the chart on the next page of important words or phrases. You don't have to understand the meanings of them, just record them by chapter and verse. By the end of your study of Ephesians, you will be able to look over this list and be familiar with the message and teachings of this incredible Scripture. I've listed the first one from my notes as an example.

CHAPTER 1	CHAPTER 2	CHAPTER 3
v.3 every spiritual blessing		
CHAPTER 4	**CHAPTER 5**	**CHAPTER 6**

Now that you've read the entire book, and made notes, just read over your list of important words and phrases as a review. Are you ready to dig for the deep treasures of the Word of God?

What words or phrases that you noted on your chart intrigue you?

Why did Paul write this letter? Why are we studying it? Keeping Paul's purpose in mind will help us as we study. Note from the following verses Paul's objectives in writing.
Ephesians 1:15-16

Ephesians 2:11, 13

Ephesians 3:13

Ephesians 3:14

Ephesians 4:1

Ephesians 4:17

Ephesians 5:1-2 (skim this chapter for instructions)

Ephesians 6:10, 13, 14

Ephesians 6:18-19

Ephesians 6:21

From your observations in the above verses, what would you conclude were Paul's purposes in writing to the church at Ephesus?

What does Paul reveal about himself as he writes to the Ephesians? Look at his greeting in Chapter 1, then his comments in Chapter 3, also Chapter 4 verse 1 and his closing comments in Chapter 6. List what you learn about Paul below, noting the chapter and verse and using words and phrases from Scripture rather than paraphrasing.

In your own words, summarize Paul's circumstances and attitude as he writes this letter to his friends.

What impact does Paul's example have on you? Does he inspire you? How could you follow his example?

LESSON TWO

TRAVELING TO ANCIENT EPHESUS

ACTS 18 — 20

What are your hopes for your time in God's Word today? Express this to the Lord in prayer.

Yesterday, you looked at the whole letter of Ephesians and why Paul wrote it to the church. Today, we will look at the close friendships that developed as a result of Paul's two visits to Ephesus.

To discover the background of his relationship with the people there, please read the sections of Scripture listed on the chart on the next page.

Notice and make brief notes about:
- *who* he was with,
- *when* he was there (how long his visits were),
- *where* he went while in Ephesus and
- *interesting events* that happened during his times there.

Just a little help here — you won't find information from every category in every verse.

They travel lightly whom God's grace carries.[2]
Thomas á Kempis (c. 1380–1471)

16

	WHO	WHEN	WHERE	EVENTS
Acts 18:18-21				
Acts 19:1-7				
Acts 19:8-10				
Acts 19:11-20				
Acts 19:21- Acts 20:1				
Acts 20:16-37				

These Scriptures should give you an idea of Paul's relationship with the people of Ephesus, how they knew Paul, the impact Paul had on their lives and their city, how they felt about him, and how they felt when he left.

If Paul kept a travel diary, what do you think his entry on his last day in Ephesus would say regarding his time spent there?

Now read all of Ephesians again, skimming the book, rather than trying to absorb all that Paul writes. Consider what Paul *does not* write about, in light of all that he has been through, and in light of what he experienced with the Ephesian believers. Does he write about any of the interesting events you've just witnessed in Acts?

What does he focus on instead of focusing on memories?

We've looked at the book of Ephesians as a whole, we've looked at how Paul describes himself throughout the book and we've looked at Paul's visits to the city of Ephesus. Let's look at how Paul describes the people he was writing to. Just who were the Ephesians?

Turn to Ephesians 2:11–12 and fill in the blanks below.

Once_____ **in the flesh**

Called_____ **by the circumcision**

Without_____

Aliens _____

_____ **from the covenant of promise**

Having no_____

Without_____ **in the world**

How would you describe someone without Christ?

Do you remember Paul's statement of his God-given mission from Ephesians 3:8? Look at this verse again and write out God's job description for Paul.

What is God's job description for you?

Close your study time with reflection on journeys God sends you on, the people God sends you to and the mission God has for you.

What is God doing in your life right now?

> I listened—quiet and still, there came a voice: "This path is Mine, not thine; I made the choice. Dear child, this service will be best for thee and Me if thou will simply trust and leave the end with Me." And so we travel on.[3]   ANONYMOUS

LESSON THREE
Changed Lives
EPHESIANS 1:1 — 12

Do you need help getting started with your study today? Ask the Holy Spirit to guide your time.

All of this study so far has been preparation. Now, we know the background of the letter to the Ephesians, we know Paul's history in Ephesus, we know the love of the Ephesians for Paul and their grief at seeing him leave, we know his trials and imprisonment in Rome, and we know his God-given calling to preach to the Gentiles.

Let's begin our verse-by-verse discovery of what Paul had to say to the Ephesians. The Word of God for the people of God. The truths and instructions for the Ephesians are for us today as well.

Turn to Ephesians 1:1. Remember the description of the Ephesian's spiritual condition as Gentiles? (Ephesians 2:11-12) How does Paul greet these people? What does he call them?

Look up the Greek word and definition for:
Saints – Strong's #40
Greek word:
Greek definition:

Did you know that saints are not just those who have been honored after their death? Did you know that you are a saint today? What is your response to this?

> God creates out of nothing—wonderful, you say; yes, to be sure, but he does what
> is still more wonderful. He makes saints out of sinners. [4]
> Soren Kierkegaard (1813–1855)

In the previous lesson, we looked at Paul's description of the Ephesians before they knew Christ. Look back at this description on page 16, and then read Ephesians 1:1-12. We're going to list Paul's descriptions of the Ephesians after they met Christ. Make notes of phrases using "us" or "we."

The Ephesians are included in the "we" that Paul speaks of. He then speaks to them specifically. Read Ephesians 1: 13-14, making notes of the phrases using "you."

Now compare the description of the Ephesians' past with Paul's description of their present and future. What's the difference?

Do you have a similar past, present and future?

Have you ever written out the story of your spiritual life? If not, take time now to describe your past without God, your present with God and just imagine what your future will be like with God! Telling your story should always be a time of rejoicing in the gift of salvation through Jesus Christ.

Salvation is just the first of every spiritual blessing! We will look at blessings in depth tomorrow. For today, what reaction do you think the Ephesians had when they were reminded or made aware of "every spiritual blessing" that they were recipients of?

What is Paul's attitude about receiving such blessings? (Ephesians 1:3, 12)

You also, most likely were once a Gentile in the flesh, but now are a saint in Christ receiving every spiritual blessing. Have you grasped the life-changing magnitude of this truth?

How has this truth impacted your life?

Take time now to write out a prayer of praise and thanksgiving to our Father God and Lord Jesus Christ listing or describing His spiritual blessings to you.

LESSON FOUR
$\mathcal{SO}$ $\mathcal{B}$LESSED
EPHESIANS 1:3

How can we comprehend the incomprehensible? Only through the Holy Spirit. Ask Him to speak to your heart, mind and soul today.

Today, we will be fascinated by the extravagance of the Lord. He gives incredible gifts but you might be surprised at their packaging. In Ephesians 1:3, the gifts from God are wrapped in a fairly common word.

What are some common ways (not necessarily spiritual) that the words "bless" or "blessings" are used?

How does Paul use the word in Ephesians 1:3? How many times does he use the word? Write out each phrase in which it is used.

Now let's find out the Greek definition for these words.

Blessed – Strong's # 2128
Greek word:
Greek definition:

Blessings – Strong's # 2129
Greek word:
Greek definition:

Now look at a few other Bible verses that refer to blessings. Make notes of what these blessings are or how they are received.
Romans 4:6-8

Genesis 12:1-3

Galatians 3:13-14

Think about the verses above and look at Ephesians 1:3. Where do you have to *be* to receive every spiritual blessing?

_____   _____

The concept of being in Christ is very important throughout the book of Ephesians! We will list all of its occurrences in an upcoming lesson to see its full implications for our lives.

Paul says, through the Spirit, that we have every spiritual blessing. Let's look at this word. Note what you learn below.

Spiritual – Strong's # 4152
Greek word:
Greek root:
Greek definition:

How does Paul use the word "spiritual" in his other letters?
Romans 7:14

Romans 15:27

1 Corinthians 2:13

1 Corinthians 15: 44

Based on the definition given for both spiritual and blessing, and the other scriptural uses of "spiritual," how would you define "spiritual blessings?"

Think about the phrase we've been studying, "every spiritual blessing," and what Paul says about them. (How we received them, when we received them.) As believers, do we need to ask for God's blessings? If so, what kind of blessings?

"The Lord bless you and keep you; the Lord make His face shine upon you, and be gracious to you; the Lord lift up His countenance upon you, and give you peace." Numbers 6:24-26

UNIT TWO
Just Like Jesus

LESSON ONE
IN CHRIST
EPHESIANS 1 — 4

LESSON TWO
GOD'S PLAN FOR THE AGES
EPHESIANS 1:4-11

LESSON THREE
GOD'S ULTIMATE GOAL
EPHESIANS 1:4 — 12

LESSON FOUR
OUR UNBREAKABLE ENGAGEMENT
EPHESIANS 1:13-14

LESSON ONE
ɔN CHRIST
EPHESIANS 1 — 4

The truth we will study today is immeasurably more than we can fathom! Pray with anticipation that the Holy Spirit will help you know and experience this truth deep in your soul.

There are two phrases in Ephesians 1:3 that will be used repeatedly throughout Paul's letter. One is "heavenly places" and the other phrase is "in Christ."

Understanding what it means to be in Christ is crucial to us as believers. Understanding this phrase often makes the difference between being a defeated, carnal Christian and being a victorious, Spirit -filled Christian living an abundant life. Let's find out more!

Write out every phrase in Ephesians that uses "in Christ" or "in Him" (or "in Whom" when appropriately referring to Christ.) The best way to do this would be to read over Ephesians again - chapters 1 – 4, but you could use a concordance or a computer program to search for "in Christ." Note the chapter and verse for future reference, and use words from Scripture rather than paraphrasing.

  Example:
Eph 1:1 to the saints… faithful in Christ
Eph 1:3 blessed with every spiritual blessing in heavenly places in Christ
Eph 1:4 chosen in Him

Based on Paul's statements referring to being *in Christ*, what is your understanding of this concept? Complete the following phrase.

Being "in Christ" means:

Paul uses the phrase "in Christ" throughout his other writings as well. For a fuller picture of all that we as believers have and all that we are in Christ, let's continue our list. (Reminder! Use words from Scripture rather than paraphrasing.)

Romans 6:11

Romans 6:23

Romans 8:1

Romans 12:5

1 Corinthians 1:2

2 Corinthians 2:14

2 Corinthians 5:17

Galatians 2:16

Colossians 2:10

You've just looked at what Paul says Christ has achieved for us and has given to us — a description of the life of one who has trusted Jesus Christ as their Savior. Jesus Himself speaks of the necessity of being in Him.

Read John 15:1-11.

What does Jesus say about being "in Him"? Write out statements about your own position in Christ in first person … I am …

Please take the time now to review the three exercises that we have just completed that show us who we are and what we have in Christ. Write out a list describing your identity in Christ in first person, or even inserting your own name. Begin your statements with "In Christ, I am . . ." or "In Christ, I have . . ."

Maybe you've written out everything we have in Christ but it doesn't make sense to you, or doesn't seem that exciting. If this is how you feel, it's time to stop and pray. Consider 1 Corinthians 2:12-14:

> Now we have received, not the spirit of the world, but the Spirit who is from God, that we might know the things that have been freely given to us by God. These things we also speak, not in words which man's wisdom teaches but which the Holy Spirit teaches, comparing spiritual things with spiritual. But the natural man does not receive the things of the Spirit of God, for they are foolishness to him; nor can he know them, because they are spiritually discerned. ^{NKJV}

If you have trusted Christ as Savior, then you have the Holy Spirit to teach you all things. Pray that He will do so now.

If you have never confessed your sinfulness and separation from God, if you have never asked Christ to forgive your sin by His death on the cross, if you've never surrendered your life to Jesus Christ as your Lord, then please accept His free gift by faith and receive eternal life, the Holy Spirit and every spiritual blessing in Christ. Then, you can pray for the Holy Spirit to teach you all things and give you understanding.

If you have been in Christ for a while, and the phrase brings you peace and joy, rejoice now in the overwhelming, amazing position, privilege and potential that you have IN CHRIST!

Whatever your response to the phrase "in Christ" – write out a prayer to the Lord expressing your heart.

LESSON TWO
GOD'S PLAN FOR THE AGES
EPHESIANS 1 : 4 — 11

God's ways are higher than our ways! Pray that you will trust the Lord and His ways as you study His plans throughout the ages.

We have observed from Ephesians 1:3 that we are blessed with every spiritual blessing and that those blessings come from being in Christ. This will lay the foundation for the study of the rest of the book.

Read Ephesians 1:4-11 and discover God's *actions* toward us (Paul, the Ephesians and those in Christ). List them below. (You'll fill in the *when* and *reasons* next.)

WHEN	ACTIONS	REASONS

Read this section again observing and noting connecting words that indicate the **reasons** why God did what He did. Examples of connecting words are: when, since, then, because, that, according. Add these connections and reasons to your list above.

The passage you have just read is loaded with God's activity in the past, the present, and the future, and Paul is praising Him for what He has done and is going to do.

Look back at your previous list and note in the margin **when** the Lord did what He did. Some things may be carried out past and present or present and future.

As complicated as these deep spiritual truths are, they are all cause for rejoicing and praising God. Let's dive into the deep water of God's perfect timing and His sovereign will and get to know Him better.

Answer the following questions based on what you've just observed in Ephesians 1:4-11.

When did God choose us?

When did He predestine us? (general time frame)

What else happened "before the foundation of the world"?
Job 38:4

John 17:24

Revelation 13:8

There is a phrase in Ephesians 1:10 that needs some explanation. The NKJV reads: "in the dispensation of the fullness of the times."

The Greek word *oikonomia* translated "dispensation" means "house rule" or "the management of a household or of household affairs, specifically, the management, oversight, administration, of other's property." The English word "economy" is derived from this Greek word. The word refers to God's administration or arrangement of all history to fulfill His plan of salvation. While God never changes, His plan for the salvation of humanity has distinct phases. [1]

According to Ephesians 1:10 what will God do "in the dispensation of the fullness of the times"?

Consider the timing of Galatians 4:4: "But when the fullness of the time had come, God sent forth His Son, born of a woman…" Is it past, present or future?

Let's plot the events that we have looked at so far on a timeline. Look at your chart of God's actions and the 3 verses at the bottom of the page. Place them appropriately on the timeline below.

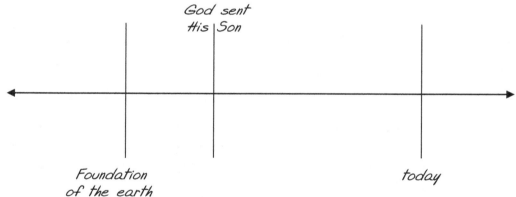

Can you see God's plan? How would you summarize God's plan through the ages based on this timeline?

The mind looks backward in time till the dim past vanishes, then turns and looks in to the future till thought and imagination collapse from exhaustion; and God is at both points, unaffected by either. [2]   A.W. TOZER

GOD'S ULTIMATE GOAL

We're still studying God's plan throughout the ages! Pray that the Holy Spirit will excite you as you discover what God has predestined for us.

Refresh yourself today by rereading all that God has done for us in Christ. Read Ephesians 1:4-11. Then look at your notes in yesterday's lesson which indicate the reasons for God's actions described in Ephesians 1:4-11. Summarize those reasons.

This brings us to the ultimate question — *why* would God desire us? The answer is right before us in Ephesians 1:12. What is God's greatest goal?

> The destined end of man is not happiness, nor health, but holiness. God's one aim is the production of saints. He is not an eternal blessing machine for men; He did not come to save men out of pity; He came to save men because He had created them to be holy. [3]
> Oswald Chambers (1874–1917)

Now let's look at the Greek word and definition for the word waiting to be understood:
Predestined – Strong's #4309
Greek word:
Greek definition:

When you consider the timeline you created, it's easy to see that God did predestine — He did determine beforehand – His actions and His plan.

Look at the following verses where the same Greek word *proorizo* is used. It is translated as ordained, determined before and predestined. Note what God determined beforehand in each verse.

Acts 4:27-28

Romans 8:29

1 Corinthians 2:6-8

There is much controversy surrounding the word predestination, but the meaning, plan and result of God's predestination is very clear.

What did God predestine for believers according to Romans 8:29?

What did God predestine for believers according to Ephesians 1:5?

This is good news!!! Enjoy more teachings on God's glorious plans in the following verses.

What does the future of a believer look like?
2 Corinthians 3:18

Philippians 3:21

1 John 3:2

Our difficulty is not actually in knowing that we are predestined to be conformed to the image of Christ, but in understanding God's "foreknowledge" or "choice" or "election" of those who will be adopted as His own. That topic is for another time! Let's face it, the Bible says that "God predestined . . . ," so, it is true.

Lest we stay bogged down in the difficulty of understanding election, let's review what we have discovered so far in Ephesians 1:1-12.

Paul, the Ephesians and believers have been blessed with _____.

What is the key to them? _____

What are we predestined to? _____

What was God's purpose in all this? _____

Remember who the Ephesians were, how Paul described them in Ephesians 2:11-12, and remember who you were also, before Christ. Think about what God did out of the riches of His grace for us all. Amazing!

How do you think the Ephesians felt as they were reminded of these truths?

How do you respond to them? To the Lord? Let the awesomeness of His calling and plan for your life, your eternity, move you to praise Him.

As you reflect on the incredible blessings that are described in Ephesians 1:4-11, which are most meaningful to you right now? Record your thoughts.

To whom much is given, much is required. There is a verse from a song that says "so blessed, I can't contain it, so much, I've got to give it away!"[4]

What blessings have you received that the Lord now wants to multiply as blessings to others through you?

Do you need to step out in faith and obedience in some way regarding the blessings you have received?

LESSON FOUR
Our Unbreakable Engagement
E P H E S I A N S   1 : 1 3 — 1 4

Oh how He loves you and me! Pray that by the end of the study today, you will know without a doubt that you belong to Christ!

Once again, read Ephesians 1:4-11 and continue reading through verse 15. We have new territory to explore.

Look at Ephesians 1:13 and describe the spiritual activities that happened simultaneously at the time of the Ephesians' (and our) salvation.

Paul has just listed in verses 4-11, in the form of praise to the Lord, the spiritual blessings that are received when the Ephesians believed in Christ. He now introduces another blessing:

The sealing of the Holy Spirit

What specifically does Ephesians 1: 13-14 tell you about the Holy Spirit?

Is there anything special about Paul's choice of the word "sealed?" See what you can find about this term by looking at the Greek meaning and root word, and by looking at "seal" in a Bible dictionary.

Sealed – Strong's #4972
Greek word:
Greek definition:

Root word (Strong's #4973) and meaning:

Bible dictionary notes:

Please write out the following verses, observing crucial truths about the Holy Spirit.

2 Corinthians 1:21-22

2 Corinthians 5:5

The Greek word for guarantee can also be used to indicate an engagement ring. "As Christ is the Bridegroom and the church is the bride, so the Holy Spirit is the down payment, the earnest money, in the long-awaited marriage of the two." [5]

Now look at "marriage" in a Bible dictionary, noting the Jewish customs of engagement (key things to look for: feast, ring, length of engagement).

Have you noticed the various references to "union," "becoming one" and "marriage" in the book of Ephesians? This is a common thread throughout.

See Ephesians 1:10; Ephesians 2:14, 15; Ephesians 5:31

What does this mean to you? Who are you? Does your status come with any responsibilities?

Paul has just introduced the Holy Spirit in his letter and will refer to Him over and over through the rest of Ephesians. Each chapter of Ephesians tells us something very important about the activity of the Holy Spirit in our lives.

Record the phrases of the Scripture that mention something about the Spirit. Use words from Scripture rather than paraphrasing.

Ephesians 2:18

2:22

3:5

3:16

4:3

4:4

4:30

5:9

5:18

6:17

6:18

We will enjoy looking further into the power of the Holy Spirit in our lives in later lessons. For now, let's absorb the fact that we are very clearly marked in Christ by the Spirit. At salvation, we were each individually sealed, marked, authenticated, engaged . . . by the Holy Spirit.

How important is the Holy Spirit in your life? Is your life giving evidence that you are engaged to Christ? Do others notice your excitement for your Bridegroom and anticipation for His return?

UNIT THREE
Extravagant Prayer and Praise

LESSON ONE
INTERCEDING FOR ENLIGHTENMENT
EPHESIANS 1:15—18

LESSON TWO
EMBRACING HOPE
EPHESIANS 1:17-18

LESSON THREE
EXPERIENCING PEACE
EPHESIANS 1:19—23

LESSON FOUR
INVESTIGATING DEATH
EPHESIANS 2:1-10

ᴏNTERCEDING FOR ᴇNLIGHTENMENT

EPHESIANS 1:15—18

We are about to study the beginning of Paul's first prayer for the Ephesians. Pray that you will understand what he prays and that you will learn to pray as he prays.

The last reference to the Holy Spirit in this letter is Ephesians 6:18, "praying always with all prayer and supplication in the Spirit." If Paul instructed this, we can be sure he was practicing it! Let's look at his prayer and supplication led by the Holy Spirit on behalf of his dear friends at Ephesus.

Read Ephesians 1:15-23. This is one complete sentence in the Greek!

In verse 18, Paul prays that the Ephesians will know three things. The word know in this verse is the Greek word *eidenai*, which means factual knowledge. Please record these three things so that we can understand the composition of Paul's prayer.

that you may know what….

and what….

and what….

Before they could know these things, before they could comprehend these wonderful spiritual blessings, they needed prayer for wisdom and revelation, and prayer that their understanding would be enlightened. Let us pray for the eyes of our understanding to be enlightened right now as we pursue a deeper insight of the Word of the Lord.

Please look up the following words:
Wisdom – Strong's #4678
Greek word:
Greek definition:

Revelation – Strong's #602
Greek word:
Greek definition:

Heart (understanding in NKJV) – Strong's #2588
Greek word:
Greek definition:

Enlightened – Strong's #5461
Greek word:
Greek definition:

Rewrite verses 17 and 18 in your own words, based on the definitions you've just looked up.

Do you see the priority in Paul's prayer? Wisdom, revelation and enlightenment were, and are, needed to comprehend spiritual blessings.

There are 215 verses in the NKJV in which wisdom is mentioned. Wisdom and understanding are often paired together.

What do you learn from the following verses?
Exodus 28:3

Deuteronomy 4:6

Job 28:18

Psalm 51:6

Luke 21:15

Now look at 1 Corinthians 1:18-25 and summarize this passage. What does it tell you about wisdom?

What does Paul say he preaches? What are the reactions of the Jews, Greeks and believers?

Look at his closing point in this section – 1 Corinthians 1:30. Fill in the blanks below.

of _____

we are _____   _____

who became for us _____ **from God.**

Look up and write out Colossians 2:3.

If you are in Christ (you are), and Christ is in you (He is), then you have the wisdom of God in you!

James, in his letter to the early church, tells us that if anyone lacks wisdom, he should ask of God who will give it liberally. Considering the verses we have just looked at in Ephesians, 1 Corinthians and Colossians, how would you say that we get the wisdom that we ask for?

Looking at Ephesians again, we see Paul not only prays for wisdom but for revelation. What do the following passages tell us about the hidden things of the Lord — how they are understood and how to have spiritual sight?

Daniel 2:22

Amos 3:7

Luke 10:21–24

Even as we pray for revelation, it is important to remember the truth of Deuteronomy 29:29. What should you keep in mind, and what attitude does that prompt in you toward the Lord?

Turn back to Ephesians 1:17. Paul prays that God will give the spirit of wisdom and revelation in….. what?

This word – knowledge – is not *eidenai,* not factual knowledge. Please find the meaning of the word used in Ephesians 1:17.

Knowledge – Strong's #1922
Greek word:
Greek Definition:

Do you want to know the God of our Lord Jesus Christ, the Father of glory? We know God the Father through knowing the Son. Do you want to know Christ – your Savior, your Friend, your Bridegroom and your Lord? Do you want to know Him deeply, intimately, experientially? Do you want to hear Him speak to you by His Spirit? This relationship with Christ comes through seeking Him in prayer, as Paul shows us.

> The yearning to know what cannot be known, to comprehend the Incomprehensible, to touch and taste the Unapproachable, arises from the image of God in the nature of man. Deep calleth unto deep, and though polluted and landlocked by the mighty disaster theologians call the Fall, the soul senses its origin and longs to return to its Source. How can this be realized? The answer of the Bible is simply "through Jesus Christ our Lord." In Christ and by Christ, God effects complete self-disclosure, although He shows Himself not to reason but to faith and love.[1]
>
> A.W. TOZER

Please spend some time praying now for wisdom, revelation and enlightenment that will enable you to know Christ experientially and enjoy an intimate relationship with Him.

LESSON TWO
$\mathscr{E}$MBRACING $\mathscr{H}$OPE
EPHESIANS 1:17 — 18

There's more to Paul's prayer! Will you trust the Holy Spirit to enlighten you today?

Paul prayed first for the Ephesians to receive wisdom, then revelation, then enlightenment from the Lord. What three blessings did he pray that they would know factually? You listed them previously but please do so again as we prepare to consider them more deeply.

See Ephesians 1:18-19

    1.   2.   3.

Notice that the first fact that Paul wanted the Ephesians to know was in regard to their past; the second fact, in regard to their future; and the last fact, "the exceeding greatness of His power," was in regard to their present.

What is "the hope of His calling"? That's what we want to know also. Remember to pray first for wisdom, revelation and enlightenment so that we may know personally and experientially our Lord and God.

Hope is *elpidos*, which means the desire of some good with the expectation of obtaining it. Look at Romans 8:23-25. Summarize what you learn about hope in these verses.

Now look at the following verses and note the great things you can have expectations of obtaining because you are one called by God.
Romans 1:7

1 Timothy 6:12

1 Peter 5:10

Paul's prayer for the Ephesians to understand the hope of their calling would remind these Gentiles that they did receive a call from God in the past, and that past call gives them hope for the future. Then Paul prays for the Ephesians to know "the riches of the glory of His inheritance in the saints."

Before we delve into the meaning of this beautiful blessing, imagine for a moment . . .

What if you had a rich uncle, who died and left you his entire estate as an inheritance? What would you like to inherit?

Now let's break down the phrase we're going to study.

> know the riches
>> of the glory of His inheritance
>>> in the saints

Which books of the Bible have the most references to inheritance?
> *In the Old Testament books — Numbers, Deuteronomy and Joshua*
> *In the New Testament books — Ephesians!*

"Inheritance" was obviously a very important concept to the Israelites – as seen by the many uses of the word in the Old Testament. Remember that Paul is speaking to the Ephesian Gentiles who now are made one in Christ with the Jews. I think the Ephesians needed encouragement that they had the same blessings, same Spirit, same future as the Jews.

Look at these other references to inheritance found in the New Testament. Write out each phrase which tells us something about inheritance.

Acts 26:17-18

Ephesians 1:11

Ephesians 1:14

Ephesians 5:5

Colossians 1:12

Colossians 3:24

1 Peter 1:4

Finally, look at Acts 20:32. Who is Paul speaking to? What is the setting? What is the point of this verse? Who and what gives you an inheritance? (You will have to look at the context – previous verses – to determine the setting.)

Knowing that "inheritance" refers to something to be received in the future, let's look at what is described and guaranteed for us in our future.
1 Corinthians 15:42-49, 51-53

2 Corinthians 3:18

1 John 3:2

Revelation 21:1-4

Revelation 21:7

Revelation 21:10-23

Revelation 22:1-5

What will you do when you actually receive your inheritance?

*The Holy Spirit as a seal is not only like an engagement ring, but He is also like a lawyer – holding for us the last will and testament of Jesus Christ. The Word of God is that testament, indicating the inheritance He plans to give us. We are not yet "of age" to receive the full inheritance, but receive right now out of the "trustee account" that has been set up for us – the deposit of the Holy Spirit in our hearts. In Scripture, the Holy Spirit shows us what our inheritance will consist of. Our Father is **rich,** and we have a spectacular inheritance awaiting us!*

Note the phrases in the verses below where Paul uses "rich" or "riches."

Ephesians 1:7	**Ephesians 2:7**
Ephesians 1:18	**Ephesians 3:8**
Ephesians 2:4	**Ephesians 3:16**

Ephesus was a very rich city, similar to today's New York City. Paul repeatedly points out God's riches, which are overwhelmingly greater than the riches of Ephesus at that time and even greater than the riches of New York City today.

Look over your notes regarding the riches of the glory of the inheritance in the saints and summarize what you have learned. What difference does the knowledge of your inheritance make in your life? How does it compare with what you imagined earlier that you might receive from a rich uncle? What impact does your awareness of your future inheritance make on your current level of contentment?

> I am as rich as God; there's nothing anywhere
> That I with Him (believe it!) do not share.[2]
> Angelus Silesius (1624–1677)

LESSON THREE
*E*XPERICING *P*EACE
E P H E S I A N S   1 : 1 9 — 2 3

This is the grand finale of Paul's prayer and chapter 1! Pray that the Holy Spirit will explain all things to you today!

That the Lord called you is a look into the past, that you have an inheritance is a look into the future, that there is exceeding greatness of His power toward us who believe is a powerful truth for the present.

Ephesians 1:19 is the third specific prayer request Paul makes for the Ephesians. He wants them to know (*eidenai* – factually) the _____ _____ of His power toward _____ _____ _____.

Find the meaning for the following word as used in this verse.
Power – Strong's #1411
Greek word:
Greek definition:

Paul writes His own commentary on this power that God extends to us. Read Ephesians 1:20. Explain this in your own words.

Consider the magnitude of the Lord's power. Read Matthew 28:1-7 and Mark 16:1-5, 19 for narratives of this eternally impacting event. What would you say about the power of God based on these passages?

Now please look at Philippians 3:10 for additional understanding of Paul's own desire regarding knowing the power of the Lord, then look up the meaning for the following word.
Know – Strong's #1097
Greek word:
Greek definition:

Consider Ephesians 1:19-20 and Philippians 3:10 together, as they both came from Paul's heart. Think about what Paul wants for himself, the Ephesians and all believers based on these two verses. What do you want?

It has been said that Paul takes language to its limits in the book of Ephesians. Let the words "exceeding greatness" sink in.

How would you express this idea in your own words?

As Paul describes the great power of the Lord, it is almost as if he gets carried away with what God has done. Read from Ephesians 1:18b (that you may know) through the end of Chapter 1. Notice the flow of thought. What do you think Paul might have been feeling as he wrote this?

From Ephesians 1:18-23, list God's actions which are described. Look for the verbs, also paying attention to the little word "and."

With His exceeding great power,

      God _____

      God_____

      God_____

      God_____

      God_____

Now go back and put the word "and" in front of each phrase.

.... AND ....

Wait until you see this! The original paragraph of Paul's thought was from Ephesians 1:15 through Ephesians 2:10. There is an exciting continuation of the results of God's power in Ephesians 2:1. See the NKJV of the text to get the incredible impact of the power of God in our lives.

What does it say?

Are you rejoicing in this truth?!

With the same power that He raised Christ from the dead, God raised us from the dead and gave us life!

> Jesus Christ burst from the grave and exploded in my heart.[3]
> Donna Hosford

Are you overwhelmed with the surpassing greatness of the power of the Lord? Paul's prayer for the Ephesians, and our prayer for ourselves, is to know our calling, our inheritance and our power source.

Do you have any circumstances in your life right now that seem impossible? Maybe not impossible, but just really hard? I do. I won't make it through unless God demonstrates His power in my life. Knowing the hope of my calling to Him helps me endure each day. Knowing the glory of His inheritance in the saints gives me a great future to look forward to, and I keep pressing on.

Well, we've covered chapter 1 of Ephesians! I hope that you were encouraged and amazed at how God has blessed us with every spiritual blessing in Christ!

LESSON FOUR
INVESTIGATING DEATH
EPHESIANS 2:1 — 10

Remember, we can't truly understand God's Word unless the Holy Spirit teaches us. Pray for the Spirit to reveal to you the meaning of what you are about to study.

We've already had an exciting taste of what's to come in chapter 2. We were made alive by the power of God. The truths of this chapter point out the differences in our lives before being in Christ and after being made alive in Christ.

As Paul speaks to the Ephesians as Gentiles, remember that you also, unless you have a Jewish heritage, were once "Gentiles in the flesh."

May the study of this chapter bring about tremendous thanksgiving to the Lord for His incredible rescue of us. First, we will try to gain a true perspective of our spiritual predicament when we were without Christ, then we will see how God in His grace saved us through Jesus Christ.

Read all of Ephesians 2 at this time. Remember, just read the Scripture, you don't have to understand everything you read.

O the depth of the riches both of the wisdom and knowledge of God! This chapter teaches us so much! The first verse tells us that God made us alive in Christ, and the last verse tells us that we are being built together for a dwelling place of God in the Spirit. These are spiritual truths that we are to believe, love and live!

Read Chapter 2 of Ephesians again. It will be helpful to make a chart listing what you've just read about. Fill in the two columns below using every description and reference from the whole chapter that is applicable to the headings.

Before Christ	In Christ

Did you know that when you were born into this world, you were breathing and your heart was beating, but you were dead? We might just as well have been placed in a morgue rather than a nursery as far as our spiritual state was concerned. Realizing this is life changing! Kind of like "waking up from the dead!" We're going to look at a very familiar story to see how the Bible explains death.

Read Genesis 2:15-17.
What was the Lord's command, and what would be the consequence of disobedience?

Now read Genesis 3:1-10.
Did Eve clearly understand the consequence of eating the fruit?

What did the serpent (Satan) say regarding the consequence of eating the fruit? (v.4)

How did the disobedience of Adam and Eve affect their relationship with God? (v.8,10)

This passage does not demonstrate a physical death as the consequence of Adam and Eve's sin. But we will see in the following passages of Scripture that spiritual death occurred at that time.

Turn to and read Romans 5:12-14. How did death enter the world and through whom?

Turn to and read 1 Corinthians 15:22. What is the state of all mankind?

Now look at the chart you made – our condition before Christ. Think about Adam and Eve hiding in the garden. What similarities do you see between Adam and Eve and someone without Christ?

How would you explain to a non-Christian the reality that they are spiritually dead?

After Paul's description of our lives before Christ, he makes a crucial statement with just two words:

BUT GOD

You know what's coming! Just reflect on your previous "deadness" until we continue with our study next week! You'll be so glad to live again!

UNIT FOUR
ABOUT ABOUT GRACE

LESSON ONE
THE GRACE OF GOD
EPHESIANS 2:4—10

LESSON TWO
THE RICHES OF GRACE
EPHESIANS 2:4-10

LESSON THREE
GRACE AND FAITH
EPHESIANS 2:4—10

LESSON FOUR
GATHERED BY GRACE
EPHESIANS 2:11-18

L E S S O N   O N E
THE *G*RACE OF *G*OD
E P H E S I A N S   2 : 4 — 1 0

Just pray...the Lord knows what you need as you study His Word today, and His grace is sufficient.

Our God is amazing! He has demonstrated the greatness of His own character by rescuing us from the terrible state we were in.

Read Ephesians 2:4-10 and note what you see that corresponds to the following headings:

God's Nature / Character	God's Actions Toward Us

Praise the Lord for Who He is! Take time to bow before Him and worship Him now.

We are looking at a passage that is probably very familiar to you. But it is one of the most foundational, crucial passages in Scripture for us to know, understand and believe.

Read Ephesians 2:4-10 again, out loud and slowly.

Now read through it again, looking for repeated words or phrases. You should mark, circle or highlight them. Repeated words may be the same word in a different form (i.e.: book, books; walk, walked). Also note the repetition through the use of pronouns. (Here's a little hint: I recommend using seven different colors!)

NKJV 4But God, who is rich in mercy, because of His great love with which He loved us, 5even when we were dead in trespasses, made us alive together with Christ (by grace you have been saved), 6and raised us up together, and made *us* sit together in the heavenly places in Christ Jesus, 7that in the ages to come He might show the exceeding riches of His grace in His kindness toward us in Christ Jesus. 8For by grace you have been saved through faith, and that not of yourselves; it is the gift of God, 9not of works, lest anyone should boast. 10For we are His workmanship, created in Christ Jesus for good works, which God prepared beforehand that we should walk in them.

List the repeated words or phrases found and the number of times they were repeated:

Repetition is one way an author emphasizes a point or concept. What can you learn from observing the words repeated by Paul in this passage? Consider the following questions:

Who is this passage about?

What specifically is this passage about?

Why was this action demonstrated?

How was this action demonstrated?

*Two words that stand out to me as I see them repeated are **grace** and **Christ Jesus**. And one whole phrase is repeated! It's the pivotal verse for our whole life.*

What is it?

Amazing Grace!!!   In tomorrow's study, we're going to dig for understanding of God's saving grace – that gift of His which brings salvation. The topic of grace is very broad, with more than one definition for grace as you will see when you look up the word. For now, we are concentrating our study on how God's grace saves us and gives us new life.

Find both the Hebrew and the Greek words and definitions for grace. Compare the meanings.
Grace – Strong's #2580
Hebrew word:
Hebrew definition:

Grace – Strong's #5485
Greek word:
Greek definition:

The word grace is mentioned throughout the Old Testament. But only a few of the references actually mention people receiving grace from the Lord. Look at the following verses to see who they were:

Genesis 6:8

Exodus 33:12-13

Judges 6:14-18

The other references in the Old Testament show us that these people of God had a need for grace and asked for it.

Lot asked angels for grace.

Jacob asked Esau for it.

Shechem asked Jacob for it.

Joseph asked Potiphar.

The twelve brothers asked their brother Joseph.

Jacob asked his son Joseph for grace.

Joseph asked Pharaoh.

Ruth asked Boaz.

Hannah asked the priest Eli for it.

David received grace from Jonathan.

Joab received grace from King David.

The servant Ziba received grace from King David.

King Ahasuerus bestowed grace upon Esther by making her queen.

Ezra 9:8 and Jeremiah 31:2 refer to how the Israelites received the grace of God

as they wandered in the wilderness.

In Psalm 45:2, you'll find a prophecy which has been fulfilled according to Luke 4:22 – what is it?

In Proverbs, grace comes from heeding instruction and wisdom. The final reference to grace in the Old Testament is prophecy yet to be fulfilled.

Look at Zechariah 12:10 and describe what you learn about grace from this scripture.

We've taken a little time to look at the Old Testament references to grace to have a backdrop for grace as we know it now from the New Testament. Look at page 50, at your chart from Ephesians 2, **Before Christ,** and think about how desperate our Old Testament ancestors were for grace. Can you put yourself in their sandals and robes for a moment? What was their life like without the grace of God through Jesus Christ?

Job described how it felt in his book – Chapter 9. See especially verses 32-35. How would Job say it today?

Remember those two little words from Ephesians 2:4 that made a crucial statement and changed history?

_____   _____

In the dispensation of the fullness of the times, God sent Jesus into the world, full of grace and truth, that we might receive grace upon grace. "For the law was given through Moses, but grace and truth came through Jesus Christ." John 1:17

What is your perspective on the grace of God at this point in our study?

LESSON TWO
THE *R*ICHES OF *G*RACE
EPHESIANS 2:4 — 10

Draw near to the throne of grace, and spend a moment in prayer before beginning your study today.

Yesterday, we looked at the grace of God as seen in the Old Testament. Let's spend some time today focusing on the grace of God described in the New Testament. The word grace is used in every New Testament book except Matthew, Mark, 1 and 3 John.

In the book of Ephesians, it is used 12 times in six chapters, only second to the book of Romans, where it is mentioned 20 times, but that's over 16 chapters! So this short book of Ephesians is rich in grace!

In Acts, you will see the grace of God in action saving souls and making disciples.

Read the following scriptures and note what you learn.
Act 15:11

Acts 18:27

Acts 20:24

In Romans, we receive much of our doctrinal teaching about saving grace, which parallels our main verse of study in Ephesians at this point.

Look up the following verses, making notes of the truths they teach about grace. Then look at Ephesians 2:4-10 for similar teachings.

<u>ROMANS</u>   <u>EPHESIANS 2:4-10</u>

Romans 3:24

Romans 4:4

Romans 4:16

Romans 5:15

Romans 5:20

Romans 11:5-6

Based on our study yesterday and so far today, how would you explain grace to the world?

Why do we need it?

Is it hard to understand?

Why do people reject it?

There are 43 other references in the New Testament which pair "grace" and "Jesus Christ." Using a Bible software program, I can scroll through them very easily. Seeing them one after the other definitely sends a message! God has demonstrated His grace through Jesus. There is no other name by which we are saved! From the "beginning" to the very "end" grace is in and from and through Christ.

See it for yourself in the following verses! Make notes of what you observe.
John 1:1, 14

1 Corinthians 1:4

2 Corinthians 8:9

2 Thessalonians 2:16

1 Timothy 1:14

2 Timothy 1:9

Revelation 22:21

We've studied and realized that we were dead in our sin and trespasses and had no life in ourselves to help ourselves. We've studied that grace comes from God through the person of Jesus Christ.. We'll study tomorrow that any attempt at pleasing God through good works is in vain. But we have not yet considered that as mere human beings, we are wretched, as in the first line of a favorite hymn: "Amazing grace, how sweet the sound, that saved a wretch like me . . ."

Let's take a moment and see what we are. Look at the following verses, noting what you learn.

Job 15:16

Job 25:6

Job 40:4

Psalm 10:4

Isaiah 53:6

Isaiah 64:6

Jeremiah 17:9

When God created Adam, out of dust, He breathed His own breath into him. Man was not an abominable, filthy or wicked creature at that time, but rather the highest of God's creation on earth, made in His very image. But as we have seen in our investigation of death, sin corrupted Adam and every man and woman after him. When mankind sees God for Who He is, the Holy One, then he sees himself for who he is, the wretched one. Sin defiled the man, the body, the soul.

For sin is of a defiling nature, it defiles the body and all its members, and the soul with all its powers and faculties: man is naturally and originally filthy, being conceived in sin, and shapen in iniquity; nor can a clean thing be brought out of an unclean; he is internally and universally unclean his heart is a sink of sin, desperately wicked, and wickedness itself; his mind and conscience are defiled, and there is no place clean; and this appears outwardly in his actions, in his life and conversation, which is filthy also: for if the ploughing of the wicked is sin, and the righteousnesses of men are filthy rags, how impure must the immoral actions of wicked men be? Man is so impure, that nothing but the blood of Christ can purify his heart, and purge his conscience from dead works, and make white his outward conversation garment.[2]

Wretched! Wicked! Woeful! Destined for eternal separation from the Lord.
But God.

Look at the following verses to see the heart and rich grace of God.

What did He offer? Isaiah 55:7

What did He desire? Ezekiel 18:23

What did He do? Colossians 1:19-22

Praise the Lord for His extravagant grace.

Amazing Grace! How sweet the sound! That saved a wretch like me!
I once was lost, but now I'm found, was blind but now I see.

'Twas grace that taught my heart to fear, and grace my fears relieved;
How precious did that grace appear, the hour I first believed.

When we've been there ten thousand years, bright shining as the sun,
We've no less days to sing God's praise than when we've first begun.[3]

LESSON THREE
GRACE AND FAITH
EPHESIANS 2 : 4 — 1 0

Begin your study time today where we left off yesterday – singing God's praise for His amazing grace, and asking for Him to explain the truth of His word to you.

Well, our study out of Ephesians 2:4-10 on God's saving grace wouldn't be complete without looking at a few more critical concepts.

What do you think they are?

Did you mention the word – only mentioned once in our passage – faith? And what about that word that is in direct contrast to grace – works?

Look at Ephesians 2:8 very closely. What words are used with grace and faith which give us understanding of how we are saved?

For _____ grace you have been saved _____ faith.

How would the verse's meaning be changed if it said "*by faith* you have been saved"?

Please find the meaning for the following word used in Ephesians 2:8.
Through – Strong's #1223
Greek word:
Greek definition:

You probably already know that salvation is not "by grace plus works," but are you equally as aware that salvation is not "by grace plus faith"? It is true that without faith, it is impossible to please God. But without the gift of God's grace, it would be impossible to be saved, no matter how much faith we have.

The following passage from Charles Spurgeon, in his book "All of Grace", further explains the role of faith in our salvation:

Still, I again remind you that faith is only the channel or aqueduct, and not the fountainhead, and we must not look so much to it as to exalt it above the divine source of all blessing which lies in the grace of God. *Never make a Christ out of your faith*, nor think of as if it were the independent source of your salvation. Our life is found in "looking unto Jesus," not in looking to our own faith. By faith all things become possible to us; yet the power is not in the faith, but in the God upon whom faith relies. Grace is the powerful engine, and faith is the chain by which the carriage of the soul is attached to the great motive power. The righteousness of faith is not the moral excellence of faith, but the righteousness of Jesus Christ which faith grasps and appropriates. The peace within the soul is not derived from the contemplation of our own faith; but it comes to us from Him who is our peace, the hem of whose garment faith touches, and virtue comes out of Him into the soul.[4]

Do you agree with this perspective?

Reflecting on God's grace and how small a part faith plays in our salvation can bring great relief! And praise to the Lord. He works a supernatural work from His own power to save us. He finds us, draws us, touches us through His Holy Spirit and gives us the faith to believe in Him.

But without faith….. What does Hebrews 11:6 tell us?

And now we will consider the antithesis of grace . . . works . . . yet we will also consider how very important works are.

Look up the meaning for the following word:
Works - Strong's #2041
Greek word:
Greek definition:

Look back at Ephesians 2:8 now and you will see that Paul describes grace as the

_____ of God, and not of _____.

> The difference between faith and works is just this: In the case of faith, God does it; in the case of works, we try to do it ourselves; and the difference is measured simply by the distance between the infinite and the finite, the Almighty God and a helpless worm.[5]
> Albert Benjamin Simpson (1843–1919)

Grace and works are mutually exclusive. You can't receive salvation from both. Salvation is not earned through any works. We've already considered that grace plus faith is not the free gift of salvation, and neither is life in Christ gained by grace plus works.

So what is the formula?

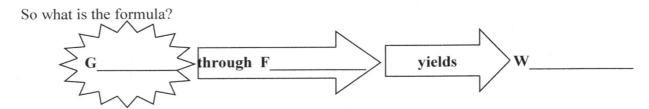

G_____ through F_____ yields W_____

Works are our Lord's expected course of action for us after we receive salvation.

Look at the following verses and describe how we should view "works."
Romans 6:22-23

1 Corinthians 15:10, 58

Philippians 2:13

2 Timothy 1:9

James 2:14-18

Ephesians 2:10 is a beautiful summary of God's intentions for us. Write out this verse.

Look up the meaning for the following word and personalize what you learn.
Workmanship – Strong's #4161
Greek word:
Greek definition:

When you think of a masterpiece, what comes to mind?

Imagine one of Claude Monet's garden scenes . . . how beautiful it is to look at . . . how it adds loveliness to its surroundings. And then imagine that painting becoming real . . . you can walk into it and enjoy the sounds of the stream, the scent of the flowers, the singing of the birds.

Your life is a masterpiece greater than that, and more real and meaningful than any painting, sculpture, symphony or song. Through you, the Lord diffuses the fragrance of the knowledge of Christ in every place. Be encouraged and comforted, and enjoy the truth that you are the handiwork of the Lord. He is the artist of your soul at work in your life and through your life.

Do you see the Lord this way? Do you see your life as His workmanship? The Bible says it, so it is true. Allow the Lord to express His creativity through you right now. Write a poem describing the work of the Lord in your life.

GATHERED BY GRACE
EPHESIANS 2:11 — 18

Please pray that as you study today, the Lord will excite you with what Christ has accomplished for all believers through His blood.

Here's some information to "prep" you before you begin reading our passage for study today. In Ephesians 2:11-22, it is important to keep in mind that Paul was "circumcised on the eighth day, of the stock of Israel, of the tribe of Benjamin, a Hebrew of the Hebrews, a Pharisee" (Philippians 3:5).

*He was a devout Jew and was completely aware of the perspective of the Jewish people. And yet Paul was speaking to a Gentile audience. He has just explained how **all** men are saved, using the pronouns we, and us, repeatedly in Ephesians 2:4-10.*

Please read Ephesians 2:11-18 now.

Paul had a specific mission from the Lord. What was it? See Acts 9:15.

Peter also received instructions from the Lord regarding Gentiles. From the following passages, summarize Peter's association with Gentiles.
Acts 10:24-29

Acts 10:44-48

Acts 11:1-3

What was the culture of the day between Jews and Gentiles? How did Jews behave toward Gentiles – "the uncircumcision"? You can see this in some of the previous verses from Acts, and you also can learn more by looking up "Gentiles" in a Bible dictionary.

I expect that there were regular controversies and contentions between Jews who were proud of their heritage, being "God's chosen people," and the new Gentile Christians who were now adopted into the family of God. This passage in Ephesians gives us a glimpse into the supernatural action that God carried out through Christ at the cross on behalf of all Gentiles. Paul explains one of God's mysteries that he referred to in the first chapter: "having made known to us the mystery of His will . . . that . . . He might gather together in one all things in Christ . . ." Ephesians 1:9, 10.

What are the Ephesians to remember? (Ephesians 2:11-12)

What is different "now"? (Ephesians 2:13)

Again, the word "by" is very important (as it was in Ephesians 2:8...by grace).

What made the difference for the Ephesian Gentiles and us as well?

Draw a rectangle to represent the Jewish temple. Then, draw a line dividing it down the middle.

Easton's Bible Dictionary gives us a vivid picture of Herod's Temple in Jerusalem which was still standing at the time of Paul's letter to the people in Ephesus. He had worshiped there himself as a "Hebrew of Hebrews."

Several remains of Herod's stately temple have by recent explorations been brought to light. It had two courts-one intended for the Israelites only, and the other, a large outer court, called "the court of the Gentiles," intended for the use of strangers of all nations. These two courts were separated by a low wall, as Josephus states, some 4 1/2 feet high, with thirteen openings. Along the top of this dividing wall, at regular intervals, were placed pillars bearing in Greek an inscription to the effect that no stranger was, on the pain of death, to pass from the court of the Gentiles into that of the Jews. At the entrance to a graveyard at the north-western angle of the Haram wall, a stone was discovered by M. Ganneau in 1871, built into the wall, bearing the following inscription in Greek capitals: "No stranger is to enter within the partition wall and enclosure around the sanctuary. Whoever is caught will be responsible to himself for his death, which will ensue.[6]

The warning described in the previous commentary parallels all mankind's relationship to God before Christ made a way for a relationship and fellowship with Him.

> The essence of hell is complete separation from God, and
>
> that is the ultimate disaster.[7]
>
> W. R. Matthews (1818–1909)

What specifically did Christ do according to Ephesians 2:14 regarding the wall of separation?

What was the "enmity" and what did Christ do in regard to it?

What purposes are evident and what results can you see from Christ's actions through His death on the cross? (v. 15-16)

Consider the tensions between Jews and Gentiles at the temple, in the market place and their communities. Consider also the tension between God and man. There is one word that the whole world longs for.

What word is repeated in Ephesians 2:14-17 that Christ makes available to all?

Do you have peace with God through Christ? How would you explain that Christ Himself is your peace?

Do the phrases "you who were far off" and "you who were near" in Ephesians 2:17 have further significance to you now?

Who was far off?

Who was near?

Where were you?

Where are you now?

UNIT FIVE
THE Presence OF THE Lord

LESSON ONE
HIS WONDER IN THE WORLD
EPHESIANS 2:19—22

LESSON TWO
HIS MYSTERY REVEALED
EPHESIANS 3:1-11

LESSON THREE
HIS WISDOM DISPLAYED
EPHESIANS 3:10—13

LESSON FOUR
HIS SPIRIT IN THE INNER MAN
EPHESIANS 3:14-16

LESSON ONE
His Wonder in the World
E P H E S I A N S   2 : 1 9 — 2 2

"Lord, prepare me, to be a sanctuary, pure and holy, tried and true . . . "[1] If this is the true desire of your heart, pray it as you prepare to study today.

Our visit to "the temple" isn't over quite yet. Did you know that Ephesus was the home of one of the seven ancient wonders of the world? Its most prominent and well-known structure was the Temple of Artemis sitting on the top of Mount Scopus, and it drew many thousands of visitors annually. As ships sailed into port, the sun glistened on the white marble and caught the eyes of every sailor. This temple was the center of "religious" worship in Ephesus. Certainly, prior to believing in Christ, the Ephesians spent much time there. Paul's comments and teaching about the temple of the Lord would have stood in direct contrast to the worldly and cultic Temple of Artemis.

After explaining the remodeling which was done by Christ to the walls around the temple, Paul describes how all in Christ are being built together as the temple of the Lord.

Read Ephesians 2:19-22, then describe the architectural plans of the Lord based on these verses.

Foundation —

Cornerstone —

Building materials —

Type of structure —

Purpose of the building —

And who makes up this temple, this dwelling place? No more aliens, strangers, foreigners, but instead _____.

These verses further explain the temple being built by the Lord. What do you learn from them?
Psalm 118:22

Isaiah 28:16

Malachi 1:11

Matthew 21:42

1 Corinthians 3:9-11

1 Corinthians 3:16-17

1 Peter 2:5

Revelation 21:14

I am totally amazed at how Paul described the Gentiles' situation according to what he and they knew very well from Herod's Temple in Jerusalem. Christ broke down the wall and tore the veil, making a way for Gentiles and Jews to come into the Holy of Holies, the very presence of God. The physical temple was destroyed in A.D.70 by the Romans, but God had already begun building a new glorious dwelling place for Himself through Christ and each new believer. We too are being built together with the saints before us.

What does this mean to you? What living stone are you next to?

The last phrase of Chapter 2 is "you also are being built together for a dwelling place of God in the Spirit." Let's contemplate that for a little while! We're going to see that Paul has just given the Jews and Gentiles a brand new revelation from the Lord regarding His dwelling place.

Looking at a concordance or word search will show many references which contain the word dwelling. There are about 15 different words in the original languages, and we've translated each one into our one English word "dwelling!" Our Ephesians reference isn't listed under the word dwelling. That's because it was first translated as "habitation" in the KJV and is referenced according to that word.

Let's look at some scriptures now.

Exodus 40:34-38
> What word do you think means dwelling in these verses?
> It's the Hebrew word "mishkan" (Strong's # 4908) — what does it mean?

1 Chronicles 6:31-32
> This verse also uses the Hebrew word "mishkan." How is it translated?
> What do you learn from these verses?

2 Chronicles 6:1-2, 18

This is a statement made by King Solomon at the dedication of the temple which he had built for the Lord. What did Solomon acknowledge to the Lord?

From these verses, you can learn the history of the dwelling place of God which the Israelites, the Jews, including Paul, knew so well. Consider their distress when the Babylonian army under King Nebuchadnezzar came in and destroyed the temple built by Solomon.

Psalm 74:1-8 expresses their anguish.

Note the state of the temple and the people's response.

After their years in captivity, God spoke through the prophets to give the Israelites hope that He would dwell with them again.

See Ezekiel 37:27.

How do these verses relate to our scripture in Ephesians 2:22?

Now look at the New Testament, after the ascension of Christ, and the gift of the Holy Spirit. We'll begin with Stephen's powerful message to the Jews in Jerusalem.

Read Acts 7:44-50.

How does this verse connect and complete the truth of Ephesians 2:19-22?

Can you envision all believers fitted together as the dwelling place of the Lord? No wonder our times of corporate worship are so sweet! No wonder that wherever two or more are gathered in His name, the Lord is in their midst. Does this truth prompt any new thoughts or desires for you regarding fellowship, communion or worship with other believers? Keep in mind also that there is no longer any separation in Christ between Jew or Gentile, Samaritan or Galilean, Greek or barbarian, man or woman, black or white. Jesus Christ himself is our peace and our unity.

> Worship is transcendent wonder.[2]
> Thomas Carlyle (1795–1881)

Let's take this great truth to heart and seek oneness with our fellow Christians whatever their race or background, that we might be one temple displaying God's holiness to all. Do you have any prejudice toward another in the family of God? Confess it, and pray for the Lord to do a little remodeling in your heart. There's no need for any of us to rebuild the wall of separation which Christ died to tear down.

LESSON TWO
His Mystery Revealed
E P H E S I A N S   3 : 1 — 1 1

Please pray that the Lord will open your eyes to what was hidden for ages and now has been revealed.

Let's jump right into Chapter 3!

Please read verse 1.

Paul's first words will get us going, both forward and backward! What are they?

_____   _____   _____

That's the kind of phrase that tells us to look back . . . what is "this reason?" To what is Paul referring? You will need to go back as far as Ephesians 2:11 to get the whole picture. In the past two lessons, we studied this complete passage, so you should only summarize the main point that Paul has just made.

The reason:

Look again at Ephesians 3:1. Paul begins to tell us something, but actually gives us a summary himself of what he has just explained in Ephesians 2:11-22.

Read through all of Chapter 3 now, noticing his flow of thought, and where he picks up again with "for this reason."

I love a mystery! I love to try to figure it out and can become frustrated if I can't. God kept His own mystery hidden for many years, and then "in the dispensation of the fullness of the times," He chose to reveal it. Finding the mystery revealed in Ephesians will be one of our exciting moments.

Underline, highlight or mark in some way each time you see the word "mystery" or its pronoun in Chapter 3, then make notes on everything you learn about the mystery which has now been revealed.

Mystery:

> A revelation is religious doctrine viewed on its illuminated side; a mystery is the selfsame doctrine viewed on the side unilluminated.[3]
> Cardinal John Henry Newman (1801–1890)

Paul says that he has already briefly written about the mystery . . . look back to Chapter 1 and add to your notes above what you learned about the mystery from verses 9-10.

Look up the meaning for the following word:
Mystery – Strong's #3466
Greek word:
Greek definition:

Now underline, highlight or mark the word "Gentiles" each time you see it in Chapter 3:1-13. Some of the points will be the same as that of "mystery," but go ahead and list them again.

Gentiles:

As we study the whole letter to the Ephesian, always remember, as Paul challenged the Ephesians to remember in Ephesians 2:11-12, that they were once:

> *Gentiles in the flesh*
> *Called uncircumcision*
> *Without Christ*
> *Aliens from the commonwealth of Israel*
> *Strangers from the covenants of promise*
> *Having no hope*
> *Without God in the world*

With the mystery now revealed through Paul, the Gentiles had a new lease on life. They were alive for the first time, in Christ. What a difference Christ makes for us all!

What is God showing you about Himself as you study His mystery, now revealed?

What is He showing you about yourself?

Paul shows us something about himself and something more about the purposes of God in Ephesians 3:8-11.

Please fill in the blanks below as we make some very basic observations from this text.

"Grace was given" to _____

who considers himself _____

He is to "_____ **among the** _____**"**

What is he to "preach"? _____

He is also "to make all see" _____

The mystery was "hidden" (when) _____

The mystery was "hidden" (where) _____

Now, what is to "be made known"? _____

And it is to "be made known by" _____

And it is to "be made known to"_____

And this is all "according to" _____

Look at Ephesians 1:4 and 1:11, 12 for a fuller understanding of God's eternal purpose:

That we should be _____

That we obtain an _____

That we should be _____

*2 Corinthians 1:20 says, "For all the promises of God in Him (Christ) are **Yes**, and in Him **Amen** to the glory of God through us." All of God's eternal purposes are accomplished in and through Christ.*

What is God doing in your life right now? What purposes does He have for you? How will He accomplish His purposes in your life? Spend some time with your Lord right now – hearing His purposes for you and acknowledging that His promises are *yes* in Christ. Record your reflections here.

ℋis 𝒲isdom 𝒟isplayed

E P H E S I A N S   3 : 1 0 — 1 3

He is the Spirit of wisdom and understanding. Rely on Him for your study today.

An important truth out of today's passage is that God wants to display His manifold wisdom through us, the church.

Please read Ephesians 3:10-13, then look up the Greek word below. You should find God's wisdom described in a unique way.

Manifold - Strong's # 4182
Greek word:
Greek definition:

Ephesians 3:10 says that God displays His own wisdom to "principalities and powers in the heavenly places." Consider that God is showing His own power, wisdom, sovereignty and majesty through the body of Christ – on display for all angels including the fallen ones. There is a spiritual realm that we cannot see, watching us. This theme is repeated throughout the book of Ephesians, and we will look at this truth again later.

Ephesians 3:12 contains a word that Paul used previously in Chapter 2, and which should remind us of the temple, now open and accessible to all. Fill in the following blanks as we reflect on the great privilege we have as a result of our relationship with Christ.

…in Christ… we have _____ and _____
with _____ through faith in Him.

Look at the following verses and make notes as you learn more about our incredible access to extraordinary places. To whom, to what and how do we have such access?

Hebrews 4:16

Hebrews 10:19-22

What special place would you like to have a free pass into? The White House? Buckingham Palace? First class on American Airlines? I know that you would agree that these places don't hold a candle to the throne room of the King of Kings. But if you did have free access into the White House, wouldn't you go there? Often? Would you be comfortable there? Would you expect the president to speak to you, to know you and to spend time with you? We have so much more in our access to the Lord!

Describe your visits to the Holy of Holies, the throne of Grace, the secret place where you meet with the Lord.

Paul closes this section in Ephesians 3:13 with a request to the Ephesians to not be troubled or lose heart at his "tribulations or sufferings."

To what might he be referring?

What is his reason for the Ephesians to not be troubled about his situation? Don't forget to consider the word "therefore." (What's it there for?)

As we have studied this passage so far, we have gained an understanding of the mystery of the Jews and Gentiles being made into one body, the church. But we have also been able to learn a few things about the apostle Paul.

What have you gleaned regarding his perspective on his own calling to preach to the Gentiles?

The Message *gives us a modern paraphrase of this passage of scripture. Read it to gain more insight into Paul's personal perspective.*

This is why I, Paul, am in jail for Christ, having taken up the cause of you outsiders, so-called. I take it that you're familiar with the part I was given in God's plan for including everybody. I got the inside story on this from God Himself, as I just wrote you in brief.

As you read over what I have written to you, you'll be able to see for yourselves into the mystery of Christ. None of our ancestors understood this. Only in our time has it been made clear by God's Spirit through His holy apostles and prophets of this new order. The mystery is that people who have never heard of God and those who have heard of Him all their lives (what I've been calling outsiders and insiders) stand on the same ground before God. They get the same offer, same help, and same promises in Christ Jesus. The Message is accessible and welcoming to everyone, across the board.

This is my life work: helping people understand and respond to this Message. It came as a sheer gift to me, a real surprise, God handling all the details. When it came to presenting the Message to people who had no background in God's way, I was the least qualified of any of the available Christians. God saw to it that I was equipped, but you can be sure that it had nothing to do with my natural abilities.

And so here I am, preaching and writing about things that are way over my head, the inexhaustible riches and generosity of Christ. My task is to bring out in the open and make plain what God, who created all this in the first place, has been doing in secret and behind the scenes all along. Through Christians like yourselves gathered in churches, this extraordinary plan of God is becoming known and talked about even among the angels!

All this is proceeding along lines planned all along by God and then executed in Christ Jesus. When we trust in Him, we're free to say whatever needs to be said, bold to go wherever we need to go. So don't let my present trouble on your behalf get you down. Be proud!

We are each called by God to be His servant in some way.

How are you serving the Lord? How does Paul's example impact you?

*In the previous lesson and this one, we looked intently at Ephesians 3:1-13. We looked at **what** the mystery is, to **whom** and **when** it was revealed, **who** it affects, **where** Paul was as a result of the mystery, and **why** God carried it out. Let's think about **how** this mystery applies to our lives.*

Were there any new truths which were brought to light through your study so far?

Are there any areas in your own thinking or actions which do not reflect the truths we have just looked at?

His Spirit in the Inner Man

EPHESIANS 3:14—16

Pray for an exciting work of the Lord in your soul today as you study His truth.

Ephesians 3:1-13 which we have just studied gives the "reason" for Paul's prayer. Very briefly, just to get into the context, summarize what the reason is for Paul's upcoming prayer.

I expect that you think we have repeated the explanation of the mystery over and over again! But don't forget that you are one of the Gentiles who received the blessing of this mystery! Your very life in Christ, salvation, relationship with God and future home in heaven are because God has grafted us into His family with His chosen people, the Jews.

Remember that Paul started to pray in Ephesians 3:1 but digressed into explanation. He's picking up where he left off.

Please read Ephesians 3: 14-19 aloud.

What version of the Bible are you reading? Did you have a chance to stop and take a breath? In the Greek, these verses are one long sentence. Some translations have kept it that way; others have broken it down into a few more bite-sized sentences. Either way, the prayer is rich. I am so thankful that the Holy Spirit led Paul in this prayer for the Ephesians and that this prayer has been prayed for me, and for you. And God answers prayer!

What are Paul's four specific requests?

*Do you recall the first prayer that we studied, when Paul prayed that God the Father "would grant" something to the Ephesians? In Ephesians 1:17, he used the same Greek word that he uses in the passage we are looking at today, **didomi.** Paul didn't tell the Ephesians to try harder, have more faith, study more, serve more or fast more. They weren't even to pray more, but Paul prayed for them that the Lord would give them deep wisdom, power and love.*

How can you apply this to your longing for spiritual growth and spiritual depth?

> We can seek God and find Him! God is knowable, touchable, hearable, and seeable, with the mind, the hands, the ears, and eyes of the inner man. [4]
> A. W. Tozer (1897–1963)

Paul didn't just ask for a taste of God's strength, he didn't ask for just enough to get through the day or week and Paul didn't even "ask for the moon."

He asked for God to grant according to the:

_____ _____ _____ _____ (Ephesians 3:16)

This is the fifth time in this letter that Paul refers to the glory of the Father. Record the phrases where he mentions it in the previous verses:

Ephesians 1:6

Ephesians 1:12

Ephesians 1:14

Ephesians 1:18

Paul also refers to "glory" in Philippians 4:19. Please write out this verse below.

Please look up the meaning of this word:
Glory – Strong's #1391
Greek word:
Greek definition:

Please look in a Bible dictionary and note what you learn about this word.

*The concept of the glory of God is huge. We cannot grasp it with our finite minds. Yet, Paul speaks of it as if he is personally aware of the glory of God. Have you ever prayed such an extravagant prayer? That God would bless **according to** the riches of His glory? Just try to imagine what the answer to a prayer would look like when God grants it according to the riches of His glory.*

What, if anything, do you want to pray for today that God would grant you according to the riches of His glory?

Hopefully, considering the riches of the glory of God sets the stage for you to anticipate amazing answers from the Lord in your own life as we continue to study Paul's prayer for the Ephesian believers.

Look up the meaning of the following word:
Strengthened – Strong's #2901
Greek word:
Greek definition:

This verb is in the "passive mood." That means that "to be strengthened" is something done to you, not something you can do yourself. You cannot strengthen yourself with might.

When we were studying Paul's prayer in Ephesians 1, you looked up the Greek definition for "might." The Greek word is dunamis (Strong's #1411), and was translated "power" in Ephesians 1:19. Turn back to page 47 and refresh your memory on this word, including Paul's personal commentary on the meaning of it.

Definition/summary:

By whom are the Ephesians to be strengthened with might?

Where are they to be strengthened with might?

How well do you know your own "inner man?" How would you describe your inner man right now?

Let's look up some other references that will shed insight into what Scripture teaches us about our inner man.
Romans 7:22

2 Corinthians 4:16 (compare and contrast inner and outer man)

1 Peter 3:4

Let's consider the concept of regeneration. At the moment of salvation, your empty inner man received the Holy Spirit and became the dwelling place for God. Your life now consists of a physical body and an immortal soul where the Holy Spirit resides. It is your soul that is under constant renovation as the Lord does His work to transform you into the image of Christ.

Your soul consists of your mind, your will and your emotions. Do you agree that it is in those three areas that you need supernatural strength from the Holy Spirit to bring them into submission and obedience to the desires of our God?

Are you thinking rightly with your **mind** about who God is and what He has done in you? Is there something that needs to be reprogrammed but seems to be an impossible thought pattern to break? May you be strengthened with might by the Holy Spirit in your inner man. I have thoughts that need to be deleted and replaced with truths from Scripture – what about you? What thoughts need to be deleted and replaced?

Are you desiring and living according to God's **will** – or your own? Can you force your will into cooperation with the Lord? Maybe . . . but probably not with joy . . . and probably not as a new lifestyle. May you be strengthened with might by the Holy Spirit in your inner man. I have some behaviors that need to be forced out and replaced with new ways. What about you? What behaviors need to be changed supernaturally?

Are you "feeling" all right today? You can't trust your **emotions**! They always need a truth check, which is extremely difficult to do when you don't feel like it! May you be strengthened with might by the Holy Spirit in your inner man. I have some feelings that I need a supernatural Counselor's help with – what about you? What feelings do you need help with?

Paul's first request in verse 16 sets the stage for the Ephesians and us to go "to infinity and beyond" our natural human capabilities for understanding. As we close our study time together this week, consider the original Greek meanings and cross references that we've looked at today.

Rewrite the petition in Ephesians 3:16 in your own words below as a prayer.

THE *Power* OF *His Love*

LESSON ONE
POWER IN OUR LIVES
EPHESIANS 1 — 6

LESSON TWO
CHRIST IN OUR HEARTS
EPHESIANS 3:17

LESSON THREE
LOVE IN OUR FAMILY
EPHESIANS 3:18

LESSON FOUR
KNOWING IN OUR SOULS
EPHESIANS 3:18-19

LESSON ONE
$\mathscr{P}$OWER IN $\mathscr{O}$UR $\mathscr{L}$IVES
EPHESIANS 1 — 6

Pray that you will believe the truths that you study today.

*It's time for a **power study**! You've heardf "power lunches" . . . you probably "power up" and "power down" on your computer . . . but how often do you say: "Show Your power Lord!"? How often do you notice the power that He exerts in your life?*

We spent a little time looking at the word power last week and considered the need that we have to be strengthened with might – or power – by the Holy Spirit. Today, we are going to completely focus on the concept of power which Paul mentions over and over in a variety of ways in his letter to the Ephesians.

There are four Greek words used in several different forms by Paul in chapters 1, 2, 3 and 6. They are translated as power, powers, might and mighty. Fill in the chart on the next page. I've gotten you started!

Reference	Verse	Strong's Index #	Greek Word	Greek Definition
Ephesians 1:19	And what is the exceeding greatness of His power toward us who believe	1411		
Ephesians 1:19		2479		
Ephesians 1:19		2904		
Ephesians 1:21		1849		
Ephesians 1:21		1411		
Ephesians 2:2		1849		
Ephesians 3:7		1411		
Ephesians 3:10		1849		
Ephesians 3:16		1411		
Ephesians 3:20		1411		
Ephesians 6:10		2904		
Ephesians 6:10		2479		
Ephesians 6:12		1849		

Look back at Ephesians 1:17-21 for the context surrounding the first five references to power in the chart. Summarize how Paul uses the various words for power and might in those verses.

What is the context of Ephesians 2:2?

According to Ephesians 3:7, what did God do by His power in Paul's life?

What problem is addressed in Ephesians 6:12?

As you look at this chart, you should see a comparison between the power of evil and the power of the Lord. Highlight the power of the Lord in one color and the power of evil in a different color.

Even though we see that there are evil powers to be dealt with, we can be encouraged that the power of the Lord is far greater than His adversary's.

Look at each reference to the Lord's power. Who benefits from it? To whom is God applying His power?

In each reference to the Lord's mighty power, I see it applied to the Lord's servants whom He loves, whether it be Jesus Christ resurrected and exalted or Paul empowered to preach or the Ephesians strengthened for their daily walk.

Make notes on your chart which reflect to whom the power of the Lord is applied.

We've observed, dissected, researched and interpreted the power of the Lord in the letter to the Ephesians. The power of the Lord is not referred to in these Scriptures as an external force pressing down on you. The power of the Lord strengthens you by the Holy Spirit in your inner man.

Spend some time now asking the Lord how He wants to show His power in you at this time in your life. I encourage you to record your prayers, thoughts and meditations and then look back later to see what mighty acts the Lord has done in you. You can use the space on the first page of this lesson. I'm sure you will see that there is "power, power, power, wonder working power in the precious blood of the Lamb"! [1]

CHRIST IN OUR HEARTS
EPHESIANS 3:17

Trust the Holy Spirit to teach you the amazing truth of Christ in you.

Please read Ephesians 3:14-19.

We have already studied Paul's first request that God would grant according to His riches in glory that we be strengthened with might through His Spirit in our inner man.

What is the second request that Paul makes in this magnificent prayer?

This is simply stated, straightforward, and yet, isn't it our deepest longing? Yes, it is mine. But why is Paul praying this for the Ephesians? Do they not already have Christ dwelling in their hearts by faith? What would your response be if your pastor said that he was praying that Christ would dwell in your heart by faith? There must be something more to understand here than simply having trusted Christ as your Savior and asking Him to live in you. Let's find out.

Look up the meaning for the following word:
Dwell – Strong's #2730
Greek word:
Greek definition:

Paul is using the verb form of a word he used previously in Ephesians 2:22 when he told the Ephesians that they were being built together for a dwelling place of God in the Spirit. Paul had emphasized that the church was where God would reside. And now Paul specifically prays that Christ would dwell in our hearts. This is a prayer for the individual believer, where in Ephesians 2:22, Paul was referring to the corporate body.

Do you respect Christ as one who has permanent residence in your life? Or do you treat Him as a temporary visitor?

> And what kind of habitation pleases God? What must our natures be like before He can feel at home within us? He asks nothing but a pure heart and a single mind. He asks no rich paneling, no rugs from the Orient, no art treasures from afar. He desires but sincerity, transparency, humility, and love. He will see to the rest.[2]
>
> A. W. Tozer (1897–1963)

Look up the meaning for the following word:
Hearts – Strong's #2588
Greek word:
Greek definition:

What do you learn from Galatians 4:6?

So far, we are learning that Paul is praying that Christ will take up permanent residence in the very center of our lives, and that He does so in the form of His Holy Spirit sent from God the Father.

Look up the meaning for the following word:
Faith – Strong's #4102
Greek word:
Greek definition:

Perhaps this is where Paul's emphasis was as he prayed — that the Ephesians would be firmly persuaded, convinced that Christ dwells in their hearts. We must walk by faith, because we cannot see the Living Christ. We cannot physically feel His Spirit in us. It is easy for doubts to creep in. For many believers assurance of salvation, assurance of Christ's life in us, is elusive. Doubting the real spiritual presence of Christ in us is just what Satan wants. Paranoia. Fear. Insecurity.

Is this something that you have struggled with at some time?

*Oh, thank God for leading Paul to pray that Christ would dwell in our hearts by faith! The faith to believe that Christ is truly a permanent resident will be given to us as we are strengthened with might by the Holy Spirit in our inner man! If you have struggled with assurance of salvation or assurance of Christ's presence in your life, please pray with Paul that Christ would dwell in your heart **through faith**.*

Let's build our faith on the firm foundation of Scripture.

Please record in first person the truth found in the following verses.
John 14:23

2 Corinthians 6:16

2 Corinthians 13:5

Galatians 2:20

1 John 5:11-12

I pray for those of you who may be struggling with this very aspect of your Christian life right now. Doubt and unbelief are Satan's devastating weapons. But be sober-minded. Be honest with yourself. Face your unbelief, confess it and pray for your faith to be strengthened. It was an honest man who said to Jesus, "Lord, I believe, help my unbelief." Please capture your thoughts in black and white, with pen and paper, here and now. Please confront the lies with the truth. Paul's prayer is building up to a tremendous climax that you wouldn't want to miss due to unbelief!

Lies   **Truth**

And for those of you who by faith know that Christ dwells permanently in your hearts, take this time to pray for continued faith, for strengthened faith and for surrendered faith that Christ will be the Master of His dwelling place. And thank Him for the faith that He has given you by His Spirit thus far!

LESSON THREE
Love in Our Family
EPHESIANS 3:18

Pray that you will be encouraged today through the truth of God's Word.

Please read Ephesians 3:14-21 slowly, letting each word breathed out by the Spirit of God sink into your heart, soul and mind.

Are you eager to rush in and discover how wide and high and long and deep Christ's love is for you? I really am! But wait. Let's savor the decadently rich love of Christ. Let's be still and quiet in His embrace. It will take time to meditate on that which surpasses knowledge. We are not pursuing facts. We are not pursuing feelings. We are pursuing Christ Himself.

Please read Ephesians 3: 17-19 again.

Please write out, word for word, the third request that Paul asks the Lord to grant to the Ephesians. It begins in the middle of verse 17 and ends in the middle of verse 19.

According to the verses above, where must we **be** to even begin to be able to comprehend the love of Christ?

What do you think that means?

Now that we've expressed our personal opinions on the verse, let's find out what Paul meant when he said it. He wrote it in Greek, so let's get out our dictionaries again!

Look up the meanings for the following words:
Rooted – Strong's #4492
Greek word:
Greek definition:

Grounded – Strong's #2311
Greek word:
Greek definition:

Love – Strong's #26
Greek word:
Greek definition:

Now, what do you think the phrase "rooted and grounded in love" means?

*I want to share with you that as I have been contemplating this short phrase, and what it really means, I was thinking that it meant something like "I must be firmly established, fixed, settled in God's love which is unconditional and seeks out my very best." Well, that sounds good, and there isn't anything wrong with it, but the Lord made me keep pondering this phrase and searching out His intended meaning. And what He led me to was a commentary that said this: "The love Paul speaks of here is the **family love** which is the **theme of this prayer**."[3]*

Well, that was a surprise to me! I think, however, we will find out that it is a pleasant one. How is family love the theme of this prayer?

To answer this question, let's look back at verse 15. What does it say?

And now, reflect on the first half of Chapter 3. (You may even need to read it again!) We've looked at it quite thoroughly. How does it describe a family? Consider how the revealed mystery establishes a family.

When Paul says "from whom the whole family in heaven and earth is named," to what family is he referring?

Paul was a spiritual father to many offspring. And if you remember your preschool action songs, you'll remember that Father Abraham had many sons. "I am one of them, and so are you, so let's just praise the Lord!" The church is one family, no longer divided between Jew and Gentile. Jesus prepared the disciples to handle family relations with specific instructions.

Look at John 13:34-35. What does Jesus say? And what impact will our obedience have?

I would like to share with you the rest of the commentary on Ephesians 3:17-19 that I mentioned earlier. Underline what is most meaningful to you.

> God's love is real, yet "surpasses knowledge." How can we come to experience such a love and be filled with its presence? Paul's answer is that God has made us a family so that His love might be practically expressed in Christian interpersonal relationships. In giving and receiving love within the fellowship of faith we experience and thus come to know a love that is beyond our ability to conceptualize. In loving and being loved we learn God's love is real and are filled with Him.[4]

What is your response to this?

I'm fascinated and blessed that Paul's prayer is so personal, so individual and, at the same time, it is intrapersonal and relational as well.

Look at the very next phrase in the prayer in verse 18. How does it also give an indication of family connections?

Paul prays that the Ephesians will be able, entirely competent, to comprehend with all the saints... with the whole family of Christ... with all the Jews and with all the Gentiles... with all the fellow heirs of the kingdom of God, the love of Christ.

We've waded into this incredible request that Paul is making on the behalf of the Ephesians. And we will go much further and deeper still. But for now, we need to wait right here. There is much to comprehend in our next study session.

For now, what are some tangible ways that you can express the love of Christ to someone in your spiritual family this week?

LESSON FOUR

KNOWING IN OUR SOULS

EPHESIANS 3:18 — 19

Please kneel before the Father of our Lord Jesus Christ and ask Him to assure you of His love for you as you study this passage.

"For this reason I bow my knees to the Father of our Lord Jesus Christ." Ephesians 3:14 I, too, bow my knees before our Father, on your behalf, and I pray that as we study this next passage of God's Word, you will receive understanding of the depths of the overwhelming love of Christ for you.

Please read Ephesians 3:18-19 and look up the meaning for the following word:
Comprehend – Strong's #2638
Greek word:
Greek definition:

Paul prays that we will comprehend the width, length, depth and height of the love of Christ.

Try to illustrate each dimension with a different image, using words, pictures, or both.

And now, can you illustrate the width, length, depth and height of the love of Christ with one single image? Fully dimensional, multifaceted, but one single figure?

I would be so blessed by hearing and seeing your illustrations and descriptions of the love of Christ. Our Savior is the Lover of our souls and expresses Himself in unique ways to each of us. As we share with each other how He shows His love to us, we all grow in understanding of how creative and personal Jesus Christ is, and we know Him more and more. And as we receive His love, we are moved to give His love to each other. Then, we, in the family of God, become more rooted and more grounded in love, and then we are able to comprehend ... grasp... attain... the width, length, depth and height of the love of Christ. Do you see the cycle?

How have you experienced the love of Christ from your brothers and sisters in Christ?

In the creative exercise earlier, many of you probably depicted the love of Christ through the image of the cross. That's the single image that came to my mind. His arms stretched out to their full width, showing His surrender and sacrifice for our sakes. From before the foundation of the earth to the future kingdom in heaven, Jesus Christ is the Lamb that was slain, the full length of time as we know it. He experienced separation from the Father as the depths of sin, death and hell were laid upon Him. And He arose to the height of glorious honor and exaltation as the Victor over the grave, over the enemy and over our souls.

We should look now at two key words in the last phrase of this portion of Paul's prayer. Please fill in the blanks below according to Ephesians 3:19.

       and to _____   the love of Christ which surpasses _____

Look up the meaning of the words from the phrase above:
to _____ – Strong's #1097
Greek word:
Greek definition:

_____ – Strong's #1108
Greek word:
Greek definition:

*Did you notice that these two words are related? The noun form gnosis is derived from the verb form **ginosko**. You really may not care about word derivations, but I've just been on quite a hunt to make sure that I correctly understood these two words! Paul uses three different distinct Greek words in his letter to the Ephesians to communicate and we've translated each different Greek word into the same English word "know" every time.*

Here are a few other verses that will help us understand the type of knowing that Paul was talking about. Make notes of what Paul says we know or don't know.
1 Corinthians 8:1-3

1 Corinthians 13:9, 12

What insight do you gain into the prayer in Ephesians 3:18 as a result of your research?

How would you describe your expectation of being able to comprehend with all the saints the width, length, depth and height of the love of Christ? Of being able to know the love of Christ which surpasses knowledge?

Know that God answers prayer!

Know that Jesus loves you!

Jesus loves me this I know . . .

For the Bible tells me so . . .[5]

See for yourself. How do the following verses verify that Jesus loves you?
John 15:9-13

John 19:17-18, 28-30

1 Timothy 1:14

I asked Jesus how much He loved me...

...and He held out His arms...

...and died.

LESSON ONE
*F*ILLED WITH *F*ULLNESS
EPHESIANS 3:19

Please spend a moment in prayer today, trusting God to teach you His Holy Word through His Spirit.

In Ephesians 3:19 we will find the fourth and final specific request for which Paul is praying. Please write it out below.

Let's begin our dig deeper into understanding this request by looking at an earlier statement Paul made to the Ephesians.

Turn to Ephesians 1:22-23. Who is Paul referring to and what does he tell us?

*I am going to give you the Greek word and definition for **fullness**, used in Ephesians 1:23 and Ephesians 3:19. It is **pleroma**, Strong's #4138, and from Thayer's Greek Definitions, this is its meaning:*

1) that which is (has been) filled
*   1a) a ship inasmuch as it is filled (i.e. manned) with sailors, rowers and soldiers*
*   1b) in the New Testament, the body of believers, as that which is filled with the presence, power, agency, riches of God and of Christ[1]*

We know that Paul isn't talking about filling a ship, or some other physical container. Let's rewrite Ephesians 1:23 and Ephesians 3:19, inserting the definition given in 1b above for fullness instead of using the word:

Ephesians 1:23 — He is head over the church, which is His body, _____

_____ . . . Christ fills all in all.

Ephesians 3:19 — That you may be filled with all the _____

_____ . . . the fullness of God.

There are several Scriptures which relate to the fullness of God. May they delight and enlighten you. Record what you learn about who fills, what is filled and (if applicable) how it is filled.

John 1:16

Ephesians 4:10

Colossians 1:19

Colossians 2:9

Please look up the meaning for "filled," and note all the possible (English) words which could be used for this Greek word.
Filled – Strong's #4137
Greek word:
Greek definition:

What truth does Paul state in Ephesians 1:23 and how does he pray for that truth in Ephesians 3:19?

Isn't this an extravagant prayer?!

It is a prayer that parallels Christ's statement in Matthew 5:48. What did Jesus say?

We hear an echo of this instruction from Peter in 1 Peter 1:15. What is it?

And Paul encourages us in Romans 8:29 with the hope that will one day be reality. What is our hope?

I am so intrigued that Paul specifically prays for the Ephesians to be filled with all the fullness of God. It seems to me to be a given outcome according to Romans 8:29. Why pray for it? What do you think? This is one of those reflective questions to make you ponder! Just so you know, I will follow Paul's example and pray for myself as well as you to be filled with all the fullness of God.

But again, I ask you, why do you think Paul prays for this?

Will you also pray for yourself and others that which Paul prayed in Ephesians 3:14-19? Please spend some time praying this Scripture for yourself and others in our family. It is according to God's will, and His answer will result in His glory.

LESSON TWO
MORE THAN YOU CAN IMAGINE
EPHESIANS 3:20—21

It's time for praising the Lord! Begin your study today with thanksgiving and rejoicing for His love for you.

Whether you feel like it or not, would you bless the Lord by reading His Word, Ephesians 3:20-21, aloud to Him giving Him the praise and glory that Paul lifted up to Him.

I don't want to touch this beautiful Scripture. I don't want to dissect it, define it, or dig into it. I turn to this verse when I want to exalt the Lord with my utmost for His highest. This verse ignites my passion for the Lord and His glory. This verse ignites in me hope for what the Lord is able to do. This verse causes me to anticipate works of God which I can't begin to imagine. This verse lifts me up to the top of the mountain and I wait to see the glory of God.

So I might be content to sit here on the mountain top. You can sit here with me, and we can just wait to see God. But, I've found that each time I do dig into God's word... I see Him more clearly, more intimately, and more gloriously than I did before I started digging. Anticipate finding more precious truths about your God by digging into this verse. You may find this study session to last longer than usual – so try to give yourself enough time to complete it all in one sitting.

Let's start by making sure that we know who's who - there are a few pronouns that need clarification. Please fill in the blanks with the appropriate persons (you will need to look in the previous verse for the reference).

Now to HIM _____ **WHO** _____ **is able to do exceedingly abundantly above all that WE**_____ **ask or think, according to the power that works in US** _____**, to HIM** _____**be glory in the church by CHRIST JESUS to all generations, forever and ever, Amen.**

Now, please list all that you can observe about God our Father from these verses.

What is Paul's main point in this exclamation of praise? What one small phrase is repeated in this verse? When you peel away the adjectives and explanations, what is Paul's directive?

Our Almighty God is worthy to receive glory just because He is God. There is none other.

> We must not compare the being of God with any other....We must not think of God as highest in an ascending order of beings, starting with the single cell and going on up from the fish to the bird to the animal to the man to angel to cherub to God. This would be to grant God eminence, even pre-eminence, but that is not enough, we must grant Him transcendence in the fullest meaning of that word. Forever God stands apart, in light unapproachable.[2]
>
> A.W. TOZER

Yes, hear o Christian: The Lord our God, the Lord is one! He is the ONLY ONE. He is worthy of glory forever and ever. I expect that I am not getting any arguments from any of you about this! You know that God is worthy, just because of who He is. And we must learn to praise and exalt Him just because of who He is. But we can also join Paul in praising the Lord our God for what He does, and what He is able to do. This statement of exaltation to the Lord is a directive to the church – to the Ephesians – to us – to glorify God as we see Him carry out His exceedingly abundant kingdom works.

"According to" is quite an important phrase in Scripture! According to Ephesians 3:20, how does God 'do' things that we cannot even ask or imagine?

Do you remember our 'power study'? Look back at page 83. Ephesians 3:20 was one of our verses that day. What kind of power is Paul talking about? (See the Greek word and definition.)

Where does God work His power? Where then will His actions show up?

Now we know that God's amazing works are going to show up in the lives of believers, in the church body. That's you and me – individuals! Not just somebody else out there. Not "them". But "us". And how does Paul describe….try to describe…the works that God is able to do?

Please look at Ephesians 3:20 in several different translations or paraphrases and record the various ways that God's works are described. Someone will probably ask you what translations you looked at….so just go ahead and make some notes of the versions that you use!

Let's look at the original words Paul used in his expression of praise. I'll give you some information, but you will still need to look up the definitions.

Exceedingly abundantly (*huperekperissou*). A rare double compound (*huper, ek, perissou*) adverb, used only 3 times in the New Testament, all by Paul.

> **Greek word:** *Huperekperissou*
> **#5228** – *huper* – **definition:**
>
> **#1537** – *ek* - **definition:**
>
> **#4053** – perissou – **definition:**

Above all (*huper panta*). Not simply *panta*, but *huper* beyond and above all.

> **Greek word:** *Huper panta*
> **#5228** – *huper* – **definition:**
>
> **#3956** *panta* – **definition:**

Do you agree that Paul took language to its limits? And then pushed it over the edge? How would you express the incomprehensible ability of our God to bring about His purposes in our life?

God is able. He says so. May this truth overwhelm you.

Look at the following verses and note what God can do.
For Abraham: Genesis 15:6

For Moses: Exodus 3: 11-12

For Gideon: Judges 6:14-15

For Solomon: 1 Kings 3:13

For Israel: Jeremiah 32:17, 37

For believers: 1 Corinthians 2:9

For unbelievers: Hebrews 7:25

For you: Jude 1:24

Don't forget that you are one of God's chosen ones... just like the Old Testament and New Testament characters that we know. Perhaps you would like to have a conversation with Him about a current difficult situation that you are experiencing.

Write out what you would say to Him and what He would say to you. A word of caution – this is a creative exercise, but please make sure to base your thoughts on the truth revealed in scripture.

Immeasurably more. You can't even imagine it. And it's all because you are in Christ and He is in you.

Are you on the mountain top with me? Are you seeing the incredible glory of God? O magnify the Lord with me, and let us exalt His name together! We have just studied the grand finale of Paul's doctrinal teaching to the Ephesians. In the first three chapters, he has taken us from sinner to saint, from hopeless to inheritors, showing us the width of God's riches and grace. He has taken us to the highest heights of expectation of the Spirit's empowerment in our lives. He has shown us the depth of mystery and the manifold wisdom of our sovereign God. Paul, himself, has gone to great lengths to assure the Ephesians of who they are in Christ, what Christ has already done for them and what the Father of the Lord Jesus Christ purposes to do in their lives. What else could Paul do now but shout for joy?

Write your own declaration of excessive praise -
Now to Him Who . . .

LESSON THREE
A WALK WITH THE LORD
EPHESIANS 4:1 — 5:21

Pray for the Spirit to lead you in discernment as you study today.

We have completed our in-depth study of the first half of the book of Ephesians. Paul's words were full of the revelation of the mystery of God, the purposes of God, the riches of God and the power of God. In perfect timing, under the inspiration of the Holy Spirit, Paul concludes his doctrinal teachings with his exceedingly abundant praise to the Lord. We praise the Lord that He is able to do immeasurably more than we can ask or imagine according to the power that works in us.

It is so important to recognize that the Lord works "according to the power that is within us." As we study Chapters 4, 5 and 6, we will be so thankful that God strengthens us with might in our inner man through His Spirit. In the next chapters, Paul will exhort the Ephesians to live what they believe . . . to live according to who they are in Christ . . . to live by the Spirit every moment of every day. You know that what is true for the Ephesian believers is true for us —let's listen up for our instructions from our teacher, Paul.

The very best thing for you to do right now is to read all of Chapters 4, 5 and 6. You will be able to see this portion of Ephesians in its entirety. It really won't take very long. Read it at a comfortable pace. Try to follow along with Paul's instructions. But don't worry about the things that you don't understand. Just keep moving — you know by now that we will cover them eventually!

What word is repeated in Ephesians 4:1, 4:17, 5:2 and 5:8?

Look up the meaning for the following word as used in the verses above.
Walk – Strong's #4043
Greek word:
Greek definition:

Thayer's Greek Definitions explains that "to walk" in the Hebrew language means to live, to regulate one's life, to conduct one's self.[3] We know that Paul was a "Hebrew of Hebrews," so even though he was writing in Greek, his thoughts came from the traditional Hebrew way of thinking. When the Old Testament writers spoke of "walking" in the way of the Lord, they meant "behaving" according to His ways.

Look at the following Old Testament references and record what you learn about walking.
Genesis 17:1 — The Lord said to Abraham . . .

Exodus 18:20 — The Lord said to Moses . . .

Leviticus 18:4 — The Lord said to Moses, "Tell the children of Israel" . . .

Deuteronomy 5:33 — Moses said to the children of Israel . . .

If you are familiar with the history of the children of Israel, you know that they were not able to "walk in all the ways that the Lord commanded" them.

Please look at Ezekiel 36:27 to discover the Lord's plan for them. What is it?

Now, look at the following verses in the New Testament, and make notes of what you learn about how you are to walk, how you are to live and how you are to behave.

Romans 6:4

Romans 8:1

Romans 13:13-14

2 Corinthians 5:7

Galatians 5:16

Colossians 1:10

Colossians 2:6-7

1 Thessalonians 4:12

If the Israelites were not able to "walk in all the ways that the Lord commanded" them, how will we be able to do so? The answer to this is in Ezekiel 36:27 as well as the verses you have just looked at.

Please summarize how we are able to walk in the ways of the Lord based on Ezekiel 36:27.

This is your last major exercise in this lesson! Read over Ephesians 4:1–5:21 once more. Make a list below of what God intends for the lifestyle of the believer. Under "what to do," list the positive instructions and encouragements from Paul. Under "what not to do," list the behaviors that the Ephesians were to put away. Our list could continue with the instructions given in the rest of Chapter 5 and 6, but we will wait to examine those passages later.

THE WALK OF THE BELIEVER	
What to Do	What Not to Do

We will spend the next few lessons digging for deeper understandings of these instructions to the Ephesians, but, for now, consider the following questions.

With just your basic understanding of these instructions, what can you thank God for that He is already prompting you to do at this point in your life? How is your walk pleasing Him?

Of the positive encouragements, what has the Spirit made you aware of that you need to let Him work into your life as a habit?

What are some bad habits that you need spiritual power to put away from your daily walk?

L E S S O N   F O U R
SIDE BY SIDE
E P H E S I A N S   4 : 1 — 6

Pray that this lesson will lead you to walk in step with Jesus.

Do you remember learning how to walk? I don't! Have you watched children learning how to walk? My own children's first steps are a faint memory. But we know that it's a gradual process, with many tumbles along the way. And those who, as a result of an accident or illness, have had to re-learn how to walk as an adult can attest that it is a challenge that requires discipline, perseverance and strength. God is so good to give us simple illustrations to understand our spiritual life.

Yesterday, we looked at a fairly comprehensive list of how to walk and how not to walk. We know that it was the Lord's original plan for us to walk according to His ways. It also was His original plan that we walk with Him. Let's reflect on that for a moment.

Look at Genesis 3:8-9. What was the Lord doing and who did He want to be with Him?

Look at Genesis 5:24. How does this verse indicate the Lord's pleasure with Enoch?

Look at Micah 6:8. What does the Lord want more than burnt offerings, 10,000 rams, 10,000 rivers of oil, more than the offering of your firstborn?

The last verse is a wonderful preface to the passage which we will look at today. To walk humbly with our God. That is possibly the highest and holiest calling of our lives.

Please read Ephesians 4:1-6 in several translations.

In Ephesians 4:1, what different words are used for how Paul exhorts his readers?

"I, therefore, the prisoner of the Lord, _____ you . . ."

What is your personal perspective on Paul's conviction regarding what he is about to say?

And what is his passionate exhortation made in Ephesians 4:1?

We've already examined the word walk and know that it indicates behavior or lifestyle. The Greek word for worthy means appropriately, suitably. We know from Ephesians 1 that the Gentiles to whom Paul was writing were chosen, called, and predestined to be conformed to the image of Christ. The Ephesians are being passionately exhorted to live in a manner which is appropriate to their privileged positions as joint-heirs with Christ.

What is the appropriate manner in which to live? From Ephesians 4:2-3, record the characteristics which are to be the regular behavior of a believer.

What parallel exhortations are found in Philippians 2:1-4?

Jesus Christ is the model for us and is the One who lives in us to enable us to behave as He did. How does Jesus exhort the people in Matthew 11:29?

Summarize the "walk" of Christ which is described in Philippians 2:5-8.

Amazing. And He did it because He loves you and me.

In chapters one through three of Ephesians, Paul tells the Ephesians of their privileged identity in Christ, the riches of their inheritance, the surpassing greatness of the power of God which works in them and that they are now one with the Jews in the family of God. And then, just when the Ephesians started to feel good about themselves, Paul tells them to walk in lowliness, humility, gentleness.

I know that I can apply this exhortation in my life. What about you? Have you ever recognized spiritual pride in yourself? Perhaps you have been a Christian for almost all of your life. Maybe you know many hymns and choruses by heart. Maybe you are comfortable praying aloud with others. Maybe you can pronounce the difficult Hebrew names and locations mentioned in the Bible. Maybe you understand dispensationalism, premillennialism and ecumenicalism. Maybe you have served faithfully in ministry for years.

What do you think about yourself? Hmmm. Is that a rhetorical question, you hope? No. What do you think about yourself? Be honest, and don't plan on letting anyone but the Lord see what you write.

> Humility is perfect quietness of heart. It is to have no trouble. It is never to be fretted or irritated or sore or disappointed. It is to expect nothing, to wonder at nothing that is done to me. It is to be at rest when nobody praises me and when I am blamed or despised. It is to go in and shut the door and kneel to my Father in secret, and be at peace as in the deep sea of calmness when all around and above is trouble.[4]
> Andrew Murray (1828–1917)

Now, looking back at your notes from the verses we have considered today, write out a prayer for walking worthy of your calling.

Wow. Take a deep breath. That was very personal and introspective. But praise the Lord for His love and patience and transformation of us. If you did not encounter conviction in that last exercise, then know that the Lord is pleased that you are walking humbly with Him.

Paul includes in his exhortation the instruction to endeavor to keep the unity of the Spirit in the bond of peace, and then he explains why.

Please read Ephesians 4:4-6.

Complete the following list:

There is ONE _____

and ONE _____

ONE_____

ONE_____

ONE_____

ONE_____

ONE_____

Look at the following cross-references for each of the following words and note Paul's explanations.

One body:

    Ephesians 1:22-23

    1 Corinthians 12:12

    1 Corinthians 12:25

One Spirit:

    1 Corinthians 12:13

    Ephesians 2:18

One hope:

    Romans 5:2

    Galatians 5:5

    Colossians 1:27

One Lord: **1 Corinthians 8:6**

One faith: **Ephesians 4:13**

One baptism: **1 Corinthians 12:13**

Paul's teachings were from the heart of Christ. Note the requests of His prayer in John 17:20-21.

So far, in this passage, Ephesians 4:1-6, Paul has spoken first to the individual believer about his personal walk with the Lord, and then he speaks to believers as one, the church, to pursue unity within the body. Then, finally, Paul brings this passage to a great, tremendous crescendo, which pictures the transcendental eminence of God.

And God is the Father of _____

Who is above _____

And through _____

And in you _____

Paul uses three different prepositions (above, through and in) to express the all-encompassing presence and power of God. In the last phrase, "in you all," some translations omit the word "you." God is not in all people but He does indwell all believers.

Please write out Romans 10:12.

How should the truth that God is above all, through all and in all believers impact the unity of the church?

How does this truth affect you personally? What is your attitude toward other believers when you remember that God is their Father, their Lord, Who dwells in them?

How are you personally endeavoring to keep the unity of the Spirit in the bond of peace?

Is there any one person in particular that the Lord has brought to mind that you need to take action toward, whether heart action or physical action, so that you may serve as a messenger of the unity of the Spirit? For your eyes and the eyes of the Lord alone, who is it and what action is the Spirit prompting you to take?

There is so much discord in and among our dear family in Christ. Please take a moment to close your time in study today with prayer for the unity of the Spirit in the bond of peace for your family and friends in Christ, and for your local church body.

UNIT EIGHT
GROWING UP TOGETHER

LESSON ONE
SOMETHING FOR EVERYONE
EPHESIANS 4:7-11

LESSON TWO
FOR THE BENEFIT OF THE BODY
EPHESIANS 4:11-13

LESSON THREE
DECEIT VERSUS DOCTRINE
EPHESIANS 4:11-16

LESSON FOUR
NEW AND DIFFERENT
EPHESIANS 4:17-24

LESSON ONE
*S*OMETHING FOR *E*VERYONE
EPHESIANS 4:7—11

The Holy Spirit is always interceding for you. Join Him in prayer today for understanding.

Welcome to the gifting place. It isn't a gift shop, where you will pick and choose what you want for yourself or for your friends, but it is a precious place where the Lord Jesus Christ bestows "charis" upon you.

Please read Ephesians 4:7-16. We will cover this entire section as a whole, even though it is a whole lot!

How would you outline or list the main points of this section of Paul's letter? Please make a brief, general outline as a way of getting your mind around what Paul is saying.

You've already read, noticed and probably wondered about verses 8-10. They are a parenthetical comment from Paul and a part of his teaching on spiritual gifts.

While I prefer, as you know, to lead you to discover most connections and meanings of Scripture on your own, I'm going to save a little time here with some information for you. And I want you to spend more time on other verses in this passage!

In Ephesians 4:8, Paul quotes from Psalm 68:18. Please turn to that passage just so you can see it for yourself! It's worded a little differently from Ephesians 4:8. Please write out the verse from Psalms.

This verse is part of a Psalm of praise to the Lord for His goodness to Israel. Verse 18 specifically refers to when God brought the Israelites out from Egypt and how God even caused the rebellious Egyptians to give gold, silver and precious materials to the Israelites as they departed. You can turn to Exodus 12:35-36 to see it for yourself if you would like. These verses in Psalm 68 look back at history and God's gifts to the Israelites which He provided for them "that the Lord God might dwell there," in the Holy Place.(Psalm 68:17) The Lord commanded Moses to build the tabernacle in the wilderness using the "gifts," the treasures, the plunder from the Egyptians.

The phrase "You have ascended on high" in Psalm 68:18 is understood to be a prophecy of Christ's ascension. Commentaries point to Paul's version of this verse as the explanation that it referred to the literal ascending of Christ from earth to the heavenly realms following His victory over sin and death. (Acts 1:9-11) Even if the Ephesians didn't catch the Old Testament reference, they would have been able to picture the victorious march of Roman conquerors as they led their captives captive on a parade through their city. Paul envisioned Christ triumphing over sin and death and leading believers in Him as His "captives," those now free to be His servants rather than servants of sin. Don't you just want to take a moment and celebrate Christ's triumph and our freedom to be His?! Go ahead!

Are you following this? Processing this type of Scripture definitely stretches our brain. If it hasn't really made sense yet, that's ok. Here's what I have learned: The Israelites were enslaved to the Egyptians. God freed them, and "gifted" them to be able to build His tabernacle, His dwelling place and serve Him. You and I were enslaved to sin and self. Christ freed us, and "gifted" us to be able to be built into God's temple, His dwelling place and serve Him. Remember Chapter 2?

There is quite a bit more that can be gleaned from Ephesians 4:8-10, but since it is a parenthetical thought of Paul's, so we are going to leave it at that. You are always free to study further on your own! The Lord uses my curiosity to cause me to pursue His truth. It can be a lot of fun!

And now, without further ado, let's open the presents! Look at Ephesians 4:7 and answer the following questions. Be specific — use words from Scripture.

> **To whom does Christ give gifts?** _____
>
> **What exactly were we given?** _____
>
> **How was it given?** _____

This verse begins with a little word that sets up a contrast to what was previously said. In Ephesians 4:1-6, as we have just studied, Paul's exhortations were all about unity. And then he says – but . . .

If we said the one word theme of verses 4 through 6 was unity, what would you say the one word theme of verse 7 would be?

As we study the differing gifts, it will be absolutely crucial for us to remember the manner in which they have been distributed to believers: "according to the measure of Christ's gift."

Who is in control here? Who is making the decisions about who gets what gift? How should we receive Christ's gifts? Each of these questions should find their answers based on the truth and perspective of Ephesians 4:7. Note your responses to these questions.

Now to the exciting details of spiritual gifts. Please study Ephesians 4:11-16 and list everything you can find in the following categories.

Gifts given — "He gave some to be . . ."

Specific Purpose — "For . . . "

Results of gifts — "till . . ., "to . . . , "that . . ."

How to use gifts —

It is so easy to lose our focus. Here's an exercise which I think will help us keep our focus in the right place.

Please circle, underline or, best of all, highlight every mention of Christ, whether by name or pronoun.

NKJV 7But to each one of us grace was given according to the measure of Christ's gift. 8Therefore He says: "When He ascended on high, He led captivity captive, And gave gifts to men." 9(Now this, "He ascended" — what does it mean but that He also first descended into the lower parts of the earth? 10He who descended is also the One who ascended far above all the heavens, that He might fill all things.) 11And He Himself gave some to be apostles, some prophets, some evangelists, and some pastors and teachers, 12for the equipping of the saints for the work of ministry, for the edifying of the body of Christ, 13till we all come to the unity of the faith and of the knowledge of the Son of God, to a perfect man, to the measure of the stature of the fullness of Christ; 14that we should no longer be children, tossed to and fro and carried about with every wind of doctrine, by the trickery of men, in the cunning craftiness of deceitful plotting, 15but, speaking the truth in love, may grow up in all things into Him who is the head — Christ — 16from whom the whole body, joined and knit together by what every joint supplies, according to the effective working by which every part does its share, causes growth of the body for the edifying of itself in love.

Based on your observations of the repetition of this key word, please summarize the ultimate reason that Christ has given spiritual gifts to the body.

What did your mother teach you to say when someone gave you a gift? And I'm sure she taught you to say it even when you didn't know what to do with what you had received. "It's the thought that counts," right? This is a good time to respond with appreciation to the Lord and trust His thoughts toward you because He says, "For as the heavens are higher than the earth, so are My ways higher than your ways, and My thoughts than your thoughts." Isaiah 55:9

LESSON TWO
ℱOR THE ℬENEFIT OF THE ℬODY
EPHESIANS 4:11 — 13

Jesus prayed that we might all be one in Him. Pray that your study today will lead you to grow in unity in the body of Christ.

Ever since I was introduced to the teaching about spiritual gifts, I have been intrigued and excited by God's distribution of them. I didn't consciously discover how the Lord gifted me until I was a young married woman. I had served the Lord for enough time that when I took "the spiritual gifts test," I had some experiences to look back on. And my understanding of how He had gifted me seemed to make sense. I've met people who haven't had the same experience. They don't know their gifts or don't think they have any, or they don't like what God has given them. Maybe you fall into one of those descriptions. I eagerly hope in the Lord that you will be delighted with the gift or gifts that have been given to you. "Every good and perfect gift is from above, and comes down from the Father of lights."

You observed yesterday from Ephesians 4:7 that "to each one of us" spiritual gifts of grace were given. Do you believe that? Just in case you aren't convinced yet, please look at the following references, noting the specific words from Scripture which point out that every believer has a least one spiritual gift.

1 Corinthians 7:7

1 Corinthians 12:7

1 Corinthians 12:11

1 Peter 4:10

As you move into the next lesson, it will only make sense if you believe that every believer has received at least one specific spiritual gift which Christ intends for them to express. Remember the last exercise we did in the previous lesson? Let's do it again now, but you'll be looking for a different key word. Read Ephesians 4: 7-16 which is printed on page 112 and circle, underline or highlight (different color) every mention of *believers* (include *men, some, body, etc., and pronouns*).

Spiritual gifts are given individually, but they are to build up the _____.

Is God's kingdom agenda to be carried out by only a few select, devoted, specially empowered people? Based on the references regarding each believer's possession of a spiritual gift and based on the key words you have just highlighted from Ephesians 4:7-16, what message would you proclaim to your local church body?

How can you live out the message and encourage others in the body to exercise their gifts that Christ delivered as a result of His victory over sin and death?

In the previous lesson, you recorded the gifts that Paul lists in this passage. Let's do our interpretative research on these words now. Look up the Greek words, definitions and Bible dictionary information on the following gifts mentioned in Ephesians 4:11. You will probably find quite a bit of information in dictionaries. Please summarize the specific qualities of the gifts as they were carried out in the early church.

Apostles:

Prophets:

Evangelists:

Pastor / Teacher: (A technical note here, which impacts our interpretation: the article, some, is missing before the word teacher in the original language. Scholars have concluded therefore that the role of pastor and teacher complement and coordinate with each other.)

This is a short list of spiritual gifts. There are others named in other passages of Scripture. But Paul mentions these, and only these, here. Look again at the purpose of the gifts in verses 12-14. Why do you think Paul only mentions these four gifts?

This study gives me a greater awareness, understanding and appreciation for those whom God has chosen to be responsible for His people. What is your perspective?

And more importantly, are you yielding to the wisdom and leadership that is being divinely imparted to those who shepherd you? Take a moment and allow the Holy Spirit to illumine any actions or attitudes toward the leadership of your church that need to be brought into submission to Him.

ᗤECEIT ᐯERSUS ᗤOCTRINE

E P H E S I A N S   4 : 1 1 — 1 6

Ask the Lord to give you discernment between what is false and what is true.

Speak the truth in love. You've heard that before, I'm sure. Let's look at it in its proper context today. I think you'll find the truth quite intriguing!

Have you looked at Ephesians 4:11-16 and tried to find the beginnings and endings of sentences? Try it now. How many sentences do you find? (Please compare translations.)

The New International Version breaks it down quite a bit more than the NKJV. Let's examine verses 14 and 15 very closely. Please compare the two.

	Verse 14	Verse 15
Who is this about?		
How are they described?		
Who influences them?		

The last gift which Paul mentioned was that of pastor / teacher. What do you see in verse 14 that would prompt the need of a careful shepherd?

Speaking the truth in love is in direct contrast to the various doctrines of deceitful scheming. It's been a while since we've thought about Paul's audience . . . the Ephesians . . . Gentiles. Living in a rich, prosperous, reputable city . . . under the shadow of one of the wonders of the world — the Temple of Artemis . . . surrounded by evil, mystical wickedness. Paul uses vivid words to describe what can happen when believers are influenced by wrong doctrines.

1 Peter 2: 1-2 is similar to Ephesians 4:14. Note what believers are to do.

Romans 16:17-20 also carries a similar message. Note Paul's instructions in this passage.

Back in Ephesians 4, Paul covers every aspect of Gnosticism and the dangers therein. And then he uses that important little connecting word "but."

"Speaking the truth" is one Greek word: aletheuo. Please look up the Greek definition.
Speaking the truth - Strong's #226
Greek word: *aletheuo*
Greek definition:

In case you don't have the same resources that I have, I am going to share with you a further explanation on the meaning of this phrase. Vincent's Word Studies say of "speaking the truth," that it is only found in Ephesians 4 and in Galatians 4:16. In classical Greek, it means to be true, to arrive at truth and to speak truth. Here, the idea is that of being or walking in truth. [1]

Is this the way you have traditionally interpreted and applied this phrase? How would you describe the context and reason for this exhortation from Paul?

I'd like to share one more comment on speaking the truth in love. This is from Charles Hodge's commentary on Ephesians, written in the 1800's.

Our version renders "but speaking the truth in love." But this does not suit the context. This clause stands opposed to what is said in verse 14. We are not to be children driven about by every wind of doctrine, but we are to be steadfast in professing and believing the truth. This interpretation which is demanded by the connection (but) is justified by the usage of the word . . . , which means not only to speak the truth, but also to be . . . in the sense of being open, upright, truthful, adhering to the truth. And the truth here contemplated is the truth of God, the truth of the Gospel, which we are to profess and abide by. [2]

Our study on truth with love continues by examining Ephesians 4:15-16. Paul reiterates Christ's reason for giving gifts and giving gifted men to church bodies as leaders.

Turn back to page 112 and look at the passage where you highlighted key words. What is the theme of verses 15 and 16?

I think you should try to draw a picture of this! Go ahead.

I'm thinking about the skeletal system right now. Paul says the whole body is joined and knit together by what every joint supplies. Can you imagine your own body without the joints and connective tissues? And when something isn't working properly, it hurts!

Please look up the meaning of the following words:
Joined – Strong's #4883
Greek word:
Greek definition:

Knit together – Strong's #4822
Greek word:
Greek definition:

Edifying – Strong's #3619
Greek word:
Greek definition:

At the end of Chapter 2, we considered the spiritual temple that the Lord is building, made out of living stones — believers. While the analogy in Ephesians 4:15-16 is different, the emphasis is the same and reflects Paul's teaching throughout this letter. In Christ, we are all one.

For a parallel passage on the body of Christ and its growth, please look at Paul's words to the believers at Colosse: Colossians 2:18-19. What situation might the Colossian believers find themselves in that was similar to the concern Paul had for the Ephesians?

What were the Colossians to hold fast to?

And how did Paul explain their growth?

Back in Ephesians, the last word of verse 16 in the NKJV and the NASB is one that we cannot live without. Please read, again, Ephesians 4:1-16, and summarize what we've studied, concentrating on love . . . without which all gifts and words are noisy, obnoxious and empty. Let me ask the question this way: what is Ephesians 4:1-16 all about, and what's love got to do with it?

We've had quite a few exercises to try to get our minds around Paul's teaching here. You might be able to tell that we've barely scratched the surface. But please consider what you have learned in this lesson. We are in Paul's very practical, life-application portion of his letter to the Ephesians.

Do you see yourself as a part of the body of Christ? The NIV says: "each part does its work." What is your part? Are you doing it? (These are not rhetorical questions!)

I look forward to the next lesson with you! We've got new things to discover!

LESSON FOUR
⁊ew and ⅅifferent
EPHESIANS 4:17—24

Are you ready to study? The first step of study should always be prayer.

I hope you have taken time to express your dependence on the Lord to teach you His Word. The next step is almost always reading.

Please read Ephesians 4:17-24 in several different translations.

How does Paul describe Gentiles in this passage?

How does Paul describe the Ephesians in this passage?

Paul basically gives one command to the Ephesians. What is it?

Paul says that the Gentiles walk in the futility of their mind. List all the references to the mind, or thinking, that you see in Ephesians 4:17-24. (Make notes of Paul's comments using words from Scripture.)

Please look up the meanings for the following words:
Futility – Strong's # 3153
Greek word:
Greek definition:

Mind – Strong's #3563
Greek word:
Greek definition:

Turn to the following verses and make notes of their similarities to Ephesians 4:17-19.
Romans 1:21

Ephesians 2:1-3, 11-12

Please take a minute to process all of this information. In your own words, describe the concern that Paul had for the Ephesians, knowing the lifestyle and background out of which they had been saved.

Do you know anyone who has a tainted past? Do you know a believer who "has a history?" Have you seen their lives changed from knowing Christ? Every single one of us has had some experience with living outside of the will of God. We must all guard against falling into our old ways. Paul was warning the Ephesians and reminding them of the lifestyle and way of thinking from which Christ had saved them. Would you take time now to pray that the Lord will strengthen you to continue to walk in Him and not walk in any of your old ways?

"But you have not so learned Christ." With this statement, Paul sets up a sharp contrast between the Gentiles' behavior and the behavior of believers. He acknowledges the change that they have experienced as a result of knowing Christ.

What did the Ephesians "put off?"

What did they "put on?"

I think you will have a better visual picture of what Paul is communicating if you look up the meaning for the following words:
Put off – Strong's #659
Greek word:
Greek definition:

Put on – Strong's #1746
Greek word:
Greek definition:

I hope the truth of these verses is sinking in and exciting you! Paul had no doubt that the Ephesians had new lives. They had changed lives. You also have a new, changed life, if you have received the truth that is in Christ. This truth is celebrated and emphasized throughout the New Testament.

Please look at the following verses and rejoice as you note the change that Christ causes in us.
Romans 6:4

2 Corinthians 5:17

Colossians 3:10

In what way, or by what manner of working, God changes a soul from evil to good—how he impregnates the barren rock with priceless gems and gold—is, to the human mind, an impenetrable mystery.[3]
Samuel Taylor Coleridge (1772–1834)

I would like you to see exactly who the new man is that we put on. Please look up and write out Romans 13:14 and Galatians 3:27.

Early in this lesson, you noted the references to the mind . . . to thinking. You observed that Ephesians 4:23 says "be renewed in the spirit of your mind." Proverbs 23:7 says, "As he thinketh in his heart, so is he." Paul wants the Ephesians to walk worthy of the Lord, to act, behave, conduct themselves in the manner which is appropriate for who they are. In verses 1-24, Paul has addressed the most important issue relating to behavior: belief. From this point forward, Paul is going to give specific instructions on how to behave. But if the Ephesians' belief system was incorrect, then their behavior would be incorrect as well. The same is true for us.

Look at Ephesians 4:24. Do you believe that you are the new man described here? This is an extremely serious question. As you end your lesson today, please write out your personal statement of belief of who you are.

UNIT NINE

Known by Our Love

LESSON ONE
LOVE SPEAKS
EPHESIANS 4:25-5:2

LESSON TWO
WORDS HURT
EPHESIANS 4:30

LESSON THREE
SIN SEPARATES
EPHESIANS 5:1-7

LESSON FOUR
LIGHT SHINES
EPHESIANS 5:8-14

LESSON ONE
𝓛OVE 𝒮PEAKS

EPHESIANS 4:25 — 5:2

> Prayer is the contact of a living soul with God. In prayer, God stoops to kiss man,
> to bless man, and to aid in everything that God can devise or man can need.[1]
>   E. M. Bounds

I've been praying along with you. I can't start my studies without taking time to call out to God for His help. I'm thankful for His kisses. I pray that today's study will make a difference in each one of our lives. That may be a risky prayer! I don't always readily submit to God's directions. So let's pray together that the Lord will open our hearts to respond to Him as loving, obedient children.

Please read Ephesians 4:25–5:2, then sort the instructions found in today's passage into the following categories.

Instructions About Our words	Instructions About Our Attitudes	Instructions About Our Actions

As Paul instructs the Ephesians, he quotes from the Old Testament. Some Bibles have italicized the quotes, others have not. Please look up the following cross-references and write out the Scriptures from which Paul quotes.

Ephesians 4:25 quotes Zechariah 8:16

Ephesians 4:26 quotes Psalm 4:4

Now look up and write out Leviticus 19:11.

Why didn't Paul just quote from Leviticus? That's not a trick question. It's just something that I'm curious about. Maybe it had something to do with his formerly Gentile audience. I didn't find any answers to my question in my commentaries!

Just so you know, in Ephesians 4:25, "speak" and "truth" are two different words, and are different Greek words from "speaking the truth" in Ephesians 4:15. Even though Paul uses different words, I think they coordinate with each other. His concern for the truth in Ephesians 4:25 was the same as his concern for the truth in Ephesians 4:15 . . . He says, "for we are members of one another."

Please look up the Greek word and definition for:
Members — Strong's #3196
Greek word:
Greek definition:

Keep that in mind as you move into the following exercise. From your chart, you can tell what area of the Ephesians' lives Paul was most concerned about. He knew the truths that James wrote of in James 3:2-12. Please look at that passage, especially verses 5 and 6. Why do you think Paul gave such clear instructions regarding the words of the Ephesians?

Let's concentrate on the positive instructions from Paul to the Ephesians. In case you are wondering about verse 30, we will spend the next lesson considering Paul's exhortation to not grieve the Holy Spirit. Now, back to the positive instructions from Paul.

You have probably listed the positive instructions in the chart, but just to have them set clearly in front of us, please write them out here.

Ephesians 4:28

Ephesians 4:29

Ephesians 4:32

Ephesians 5:1-2

Oh, don't you want to live with a group of people who act like that? A phrase from one of the first songs that I learned in Sunday School was, "They will know we are Christians by our love, by our love, yes they'll know we are Christians by our love." Believers really can live together that way.

Look at Acts 2:42-47. What do you see in that passage that represents Paul's positive instructions to the Ephesians?

> Do not keep the alabaster boxes of your love and tenderness sealed up until your friends are dead. Fill their lives with sweetness. Speak approving, cheering words while their ears can hear them and while their hearts can be thrilled by them.[2]
>
> Henry Ward Beecher (1813–1887)

Look back at Ephesians 4:32 and 5:2. What is the reason that Paul gives for believers to be kind, tenderhearted, forgiving and loving?

Once again, dear Paul shows his devotion to Jesus Christ his Lord and Savior. Our actions are really just to be responses to what we have received from Jesus. We love because He first loved us. His love to each of us, unlovables, will enable us to love our brothers and sisters in the family of God.

Please make this personal now. Look back over the chart of instructions from Paul. What do you need to put away — for the building up of the body, in response to the love which Christ has shown to you?

What do you need to practice — for the building up of the body, in response to the love which Christ has shown to you?

Behold, how good and how pleasant it is for brethren to dwell together in unity! Psalm 133:1

Words Hurt

EPHESIANS 4:30

Speak to the Holy Spirit as you would to the Lord. Ask Him to move in your heart, soul, and mind and to lead you to understand Him more and more.

I come to this portion of our study soberly and cautiously. Let us approach the Holy Spirit of God with reverence for Who He is.

Please write out Ephesians 4:30.

Back when we were studying Chapter 1, we looked closely at the sealing of the Spirit, which is the guarantee of our inheritance. Turn back to pages 35 and 36 and review what this means for us. My next question will be based on what you learned there.

What is the sealing of the Holy Spirit?

What is "the day of redemption?" Begin by looking up the meaning for the following word:
Redemption — Strong's #629
Greek word:
Greek definition:

How do the following verses add to your understanding of the meaning of 'the day of redemption."

Luke 21:28

Romans 8:23

Pause here to absorb the fact that your soul is in the safe-keeping of the Holy Spirit. Let the magnitude of this truth sink in. Imagine what it would be like to live without the sealing of the Holy Spirit.

Write out your thoughts.

I hope you are realizing the crucial role that the Holy Spirit carries out for us. With that in mind, now let us look at who the Spirit is.

Ephesians 4:30 says: "do not grieve the Holy Spirit _____ _____."

Please look at the following Scriptures so that you may become consciously aware of the third member of the Trinity, the Spirit of God. Please note His role, influence or action in the following verses.

Genesis 1:2

Isaiah 61:1

Matthew 3:16

Romans 8:9, 14

1 Corinthians 2:10-12

1 Corinthians 3:16

Galatians 4:6

Is the Holy Spirit the Spirit of God or the Spirit of Christ? Please explain your answer.

Please look up the meaning for the following word as found in Ephesians 4:30.
Spirit – Strong's #4151
Greek word:
Greek definition:

Jesus gave a beautiful explanation to Nicodemus of what it is like to be born of the Spirit.

Look at John 3:8 and describe the influence of the Holy Spirit as Jesus did. You should see a correlation to the Greek word *pneuma.*

We've worked through Ephesians 4:30 from end to beginning. Hopefully, you are now much more consciously aware of Who the Spirit is, what He is doing and how He works. Keeping all of that in mind, let's think about the exhortation from Paul: "and do not grieve the Holy Spirit of God."

Please look up the meaning for the following word:
Grieve – Strong's #3076
Greek word:
Greek definition:

Remember the context of this verse that we studied yesterday. What has Paul mentioned that would cause distress and sorrow for the Holy Spirit?

There are two references in the Old Testament which mention grieving the Holy Spirit. Look at Isaiah 63:10. In verses 7-9, the author is remembering God's mercy and loving-kindness to the Israelites when He saved them out of Egypt. But what did the people do after He delivered them?

Psalm 78:40-42 mentions the same events. How did the Israelites grieve the Holy Spirit in the desert?

Based on the context of Ephesians 4:30, and the illustrations of the Israelites grieving the Holy Spirit, what would you say distresses and saddens the Holy Spirit of God?

I've never noticed this before. Think about the greater context of unity and love among the members of the body of Christ that we've seen in Chapter 4.

The Holy Spirit of God desires that we all be knit together and testify to one Lord, one faith, one baptism, one God and Father of all. He mourns when we bicker and bite with our mouths, when we slander and slap with our words, when we argue and ignite each other to corrupt communication.

I thought the previous lesson was pretty serious regarding the words we speak. Today's lesson is even more so.

Please note the truths found in the following verses:

Proverbs 10:31

Proverbs 15:2

Matthew 12:34

Close your time in study today by confessing to the Holy Spirit any hurtful words that you have expressed recently against other believers, whether it was to them in person or not. Follow your confession with a time of thanksgiving and appreciation for these members of your spiritual family. In doing so, you will not grieve the Spirit, but rather, you will delight Him.

L E S S O N   T H R E E
Sin Separates
E P H E S I A N S   5 : 1 — 7

Pray that the Lord will impress upon you the witness that you carry for Him

.

This will be an uncomfortable lesson and a longer lesson than usual. God's Word brings us face to face with behavior that is truly X-rated. Let us not become desensitized to sin. Let the Holy Spirit direct us to hate what the Lord hates. Not the people, but the practices of the people. These verses were written as warnings, exhortations, strong statements to put away and have nothing to do with any practices that may have been a part of the Ephesians' past. Paul continues to instruct the believers at Ephesus and all of us today to walk worthy of the calling with which they and we were called.

Please read Ephesians 5:1-16.

Therefore be imitators of God as dear children. ²And walk in love, as Christ also has loved us and given Himself for us, an offering and a sacrifice to God for a sweet-smelling aroma.

³But fornication and all uncleanness or covetousness, let it not even be named among you, as is fitting for saints; ⁴neither filthiness, nor foolish talking, nor coarse jesting, which are not fitting, but rather giving of thanks. ⁵For this you know, that no fornicator, unclean person, nor covetous man, who is an idolater, has any inheritance in the kingdom of Christ and God.

⁶Let no one deceive you with empty words, for because of these things the wrath of God comes upon the sons of disobedience. ⁷Therefore do not be partakers with them. ⁸For you were once darkness, but now you are light in the Lord. Walk as children of light ⁹(for the fruit of the Spirit is in all goodness, righteousness, and truth), ¹⁰finding out what is acceptable to the Lord. ¹¹And have no fellowship with the unfruitful works of darkness, but rather expose them. ¹²For it is shameful even to speak of those things which are done by them in secret. ¹³But all things that are exposed are made manifest by the light, for whatever makes manifest is light. ¹⁴Therefore He says: "Awake, you who sleep, arise from the dead, and Christ will give you light."

¹⁵See then that you walk circumspectly, not as fools but as wise, ¹⁶redeeming the time, because the days are evil.

Highlight all references to sinful actions and attitudes and those who do them in one color, and then in another color, highlight all references to believers and "what is acceptable to the Lord." This is a passage of contrasts.

Please look up the meaning for the following words from this passage:
Fornication - Strong's #4202
Greek word:
Greek definition:

Uncleanness – Strong's #167
Greek word:
Greek definition

Covetousness – Strong's #4124
Greek word:
Greek definition:

Idolater – Strong's #1496
Greek word:
Greek definition:

What does Ephesians 5:5 say regarding fornicators, unclean persons or covetous men?

Please read the following notes from commentaries and look for information which correlates to this consequence, underlining your findings.

Regarding Fornication:

Ephesus was the center of worship of the goddess Artemis, also known as Diana. Artemis was considered a goddess of fertility and her image depicted reproductive aspects of men, women and animals.

> The ritual of the temple services consisted of sacrifices and of ceremonial prostitution, a practice which was common to many of the religions of the ancient Orient, and which still exists among some of the obscure tribes of Asia Minor. [3]

This fornication was common among Gentiles and was not thought to be criminal. The believers at Ephesus also encountered the Nicolaitans whose deeds included committing fornication and eating things sacrificed to idols. Jesus Himself said in His letter to the Ephesians that He hates the deeds of the Nicolaitans. (Revelation 2:6)

The term fornication was also used in a symbolic sense by the prophets Isaiah, Jeremiah and Hosea to indicate a forsaking of God or a following after idols.

> In the Hebrew language, *zanah* means "to commit adultery,fornication or illicit incontinence of any kind". Its derivative, *taznuth,* means "fornication," "harlotry," "whoredom". In the Greek, *porneuo,* (verb) and *porneia* (noun), have the same meaning. The following passages will reveal the estimate in which such uncleanness was held, and the fact that men and women given to it were held in equal abhorrence and designated by the same terms: Gen 38:24; Lev 19:29; Nu 14:33; 25:1; Ezek 16; 23:3, 7, 8, 11, 27, 29, 43; 43:7, 9; Hos 1:2; 2:4; 4:11, 12; 6:10; Nah 3:4; Mt 5:32; Rom 1:26 f; 1 Cor 5:1; 7:2; 10:8; Jude 1:7; Rev 2:14, 20 f; 18:9; 19:2. [4]

Regarding Uncleanness:

> In Ephesians 5:3, "All uncleanness" takes in adultery, incest, sodomy, and every unnatural lust. [5]

> "Uncleanness" and "covetousness" are taken up again from Ephesians 4:19. The two are so closely allied that the Greek for "covetousness" (pleonexiais) used sometimes in Scripture, and often in the Greek fathers, for sins of impurity. The common principle is the longing to fill one's desire with material objects of sense, outside of God. The expression, "not be even named," applies better to impurity, than to "covetousness." [6]

The Hebrew root meaning "clean" is found 204 times in the Old Testament, and the root meaning "unclean" or "defiled" 279 times. These words describe a state or condition that affects a person's relationship with God. In Leviticus, clean and unclean are ritual terms. An "unclean" person could not take part in worship or eat sacrificed meat (Num. 5:1-4). In some cases an unclean person was to be isolated from others (Lev. 13:45-46). As the next chapters of Lev. show, rules of ritual cleanness and uncleanness focus on the basic experiences of life—birth, death, sex, health, and food. In setting up these rules, God showed He was concerned about every aspect of His people's life and that people are to relate all things in life to the Lord.

Later the prophets of Israel applied the image of ritual uncleanness to moral issues. They boldly announced that sin defiles, thus cutting sinners off from God. The psalmist says of Israel, "they defiled themselves by what they did" (Ps. 106:39). Thus the imagery of uncleanness has great spiritual significance, and powerfully communicates the truth that sin separates us from God. Only a cleansed sinner can approach the Lord. [7]

Regarding Covetousness:

Covetousness is a very grave sin; indeed, so heinous is it that the Scriptures class it among the very gravest and grossest crimes (Eph. 5:3). In Col.3:5 it is "idolatry," while in 1 Cor.6:10 it is set forth as excluding a man from heaven. Its heinousness, doubtless, is accounted for by its being in a very real sense the root of so many other forms of sin, e.g. departure from the faith (1 Tim.6:9, 10); lying (2 Ki.5:22-25); theft (Josh.7:21); domestic trouble (Prov.15:27); murder (Ezek.22:12); indeed, it leads to "many foolish and hurtful lusts" (1 Tim.6:9). Covetousness has always been a very serious menace to mankind, whether in the Old Testament or New Testament period. It was one of the first sins that broke out after Israel had entered into the Promised Land (Achan, Josh.7); and also in the early Christian church immediately after its founding (Ananias and Sapphira, Acts 5); hence, so many warnings against it. [8]

At this point, please take a moment and look at Colossians 3:5. What does this verse tell us regarding fornication, uncleanness and covetousness?

Regarding Idolater:

The covetous man may be called an idolater, because the idolater and he worship the same in substance, gold and silver, and brass, or what is made of them; the covetous man admires his gold, lays it up, and will not make use of it, as if it was something sacred; and through his over love to mammon, whom he serves, he neglects the worship of God, and the good of his

In the Old Testament, the special enticements to idolatry as offered by various cults were found in their deification of natural forces and their appeal to primitive human desires, especially the sexual. Baal and Astarte worship, which was especially attractive, was closely associated with fornication and drunkenness (Am 2:7, 8; compare 1 Ki 14:23 f), and also appealed greatly to magic and soothsaying (e.g. Isa 2:6; 3:2; 8:19). [10]

What did you notice in all of the previous commentary notes that would lead Paul to state that no fornicator, unclean person, nor covetous man has any inheritance in the kingdom of Christ and God?

Please read Ephesians 5:3-7 again. Keep verses 6 and 7 in mind as you look up the meaning for the following words:

Filthiness – Strong's #151
Greek word:
Greek definition:

Foolish talking – Strong's #3473
Greek word:
Greek definition:

Coarse jesting – Strong's #2160
Greek word:
Greek definition:

In Colossians 3:8-9, Paul gives a very similar instruction to that which he gave the Ephesians. Please record these similarities.

I am ready for words fitly spoken . . .beautiful words . . . like apples of gold in settings of silver. But we can't think on them quite yet. Please read the following notes from a few more commentaries. Then, we will give thanks!

Regarding Foolish Talking:

Only here in the New Testament. Talk which is both foolish and sinful. Compare *corrupt communication*, Ephesians 4:29. It is more than random or idle talk.[11]

Regarding Jesting:

The sense of the word here is *polished and witty speech as the instrument of sin;* refinement and versatility without the flavor of Christian grace. "Sometimes it is lodged in a sly question, in a smart answer, in a quirkish reason, in shrewd intimation, in cunningly diverting or cleverly retorting an objection: sometimes it is couched in a bold scheme of speech, in a tart irony, in a lusty hyperbole, in a startling metaphor, in a plausible reconciling of contradictions, or in acute nonsense.... Sometimes an affected simplicity, sometimes a presumptuous bluntness giveth it being.... Its ways are unaccountable and inexplicable, being answerable to the numberless rovings of fancy and windings of language" [12]

Regarding Jest:

An act intended to provoke laughter; an utterance intended as mockery or humor. Thinking Lot was jesting about Sodom's imminent destruction, his sons-in-law remained in the city (Gen. 19:14). The jesters of Psalm 35:16 (NASB) are mockers. Isaiah 57:4 describes idolatry as making God the object of a jest (KJV sport). Ephesians 5:4 characterizes jesting or mocking speech as part of a pagan life-style. [13]

In the next commentary, I think you will sense the offensiveness and sinfulness of "filthiness, foolish talking, and coarse jesting.'" Picture yourself as a bystander in this scene.

Good Friday….. The scourging ended, the soldiery would hastily cast upon Him His upper garments, and lead Him back into the Praetorium. Here they called the whole cohort together, and the silent, faint Sufferer became the object of their ribald *jesting*. From His bleeding Body they tore the clothes, and in *mockery* arrayed Him in scarlet or purple. For crown they wound together thorns, and for sceptre they placed in His Hand a reed. Then alternately, *in mock proclamation* they hailed Him King, or worshipped Him as God, and smote Him or heaped on Him other indignities. [14]

What are your thoughts now about foolish talking and coarse jesting?

Matthew Henry's Commentary gives us a good conclusion of what we should learn from Ephesians 5:3-7.

Filthy lusts must be rooted out. These sins must be dreaded and detested. Here are not only cautions against gross acts of sin, but against what some may make light of. But these things are so far from being profitable that they pollute and poison the hearers. [15]

We've looked at gross acts of sin as well as foolishness and filthiness. My research which took me back in time gave me the perspective that there were no "good old days" in Ephesus. Our culture today is similar in so many ways to the culture in which Paul lived. The Temple of Artemis and its environs would have been as bad as our modern "red-light" districts. But Paul didn't caution only against obvious, vulgar sins; he also warned against empty, foolish, deceitful words.

What are you going to do with all of this information now? What is Paul's concluding exhortation in Ephesians 5:7?

Examine your life, your longings and your language. Are you partaking in any of the activities, enticements or expressions which poison and pollute? Please especially consider the things you "say in jest."

I feel "unclean" after this study, but I am thankful that Jesus said, "You are already clean because of the Word which I have spoken to you." (John 15:3) Let us now do what is fitting for saints, who have an inheritance awaiting us in the kingdom of God. Close with thanksgiving to God for cleansing us through the blood of Christ and His Holy Words.

LESSON FOUR
ℒIGHT 𝒮HINES

EPHESIANS 5 : 8 — 1 4

Praise God! Rejoice that the Light of the world came and made a way for us to know Him and become light in this dark world.

I love God's Word and know that everything He says is profitable. Some of what He says is hard to read. Today, however, we will enjoy His Words that are sweeter than honey. We are still in the midst of studying Paul's instructions in Chapter 5.

Once again, please read Ephesians 5: 1- 21.

Observe the ways that Paul tells the Ephesians to walk. And on the next page, note how Paul says it will look in their lives. (The NIV says "live" rather than "walk".)

Walk in _____

Walk as _____

Walk _____

How does Ephesians 5:8 describe the Ephesian believers?

Look at 1 Thessalonians 5:5-8 and add to your description.

Please look up the meaning for the following word as found in Ephesians 5:8.
Light – Strong's #5457
Greek word:
Greek definition:

We just have to look at some other verses with this beautiful word in it. Isn't it refreshing to have a beautiful word after yesterday's study?

There are so many cross-references. Here are a few that I would like you to see. Please make notes of the light that is described in the following verses.

Matthew 4:16

Matthew 17:1-2

Luke 2:30-32

John 1:4-5

John 8:12

John 12:36

Jesus said, "You are the light of the world." (Matthew 5:14) Wow! Really? Jesus is the Light of the world. How can we be the light of the world? Are you so used to hearing that phrase that you don't even think about it?

What do you see in Ephesians 5:8-21 that helps us understand how to live as the light of the world?

Creative drawing time again! Please draw the outline of a person. Stick figures will not work for this exercise. Now, imagine that this person is Jesus, transfigured on the mountain, with radiant light shining from Him. Draw the light. Next, place yourself in this picture. Remember from earlier lessons that you are *in Christ*.

Back to my question, how can *we* be the light of the world?

After Jesus stated that "You are the light of the world," He then told the people what they were to do as a result of that status. You probably know what He said, but look at it to refresh your memory and realize that Paul is just taking his cues from Jesus!

What did Jesus say in Matthew 5:14-16?

Ephesians 5:4, 9-10, 15-21 give believers very clear ways to let their light shine before men. What is listed in these verses?

In 2 Corinthians 6:14-7:1, you will find a passage that is an excellent commentary to our passage in Ephesians. Please read the verses, then summarize what we have studied so far in Ephesians 5. Make this your own simple explanation of what Paul has said to his dear friends. How would you write this exhortation to a friend of yours?

The final verse which we will look at today is Ephesians 5:14. It is set apart in my Bible as a quote from Isaiah 60:1. Paul has paraphrased, again! One commentator said that an author has a right to change his own writings. Since the Holy Spirit is the real author of Scripture, He certainly has the right to paraphrase! Please look at the beautiful image depicted by Isaiah. I think that either of these verses would be a wonderful way to start each new day!

Please write these verses.
Ephesians 5:14   Isaiah 60:1

What similar image and instructions do you see in Romans 13:11-13?

Look back at Ephesians 2:1. What truth does Paul reiterate in Ephesians 5:14?

There is one more passage in Romans that I just have to ask you to look at. It is loaded with truth that changed my life. I am ecstatic about what our Father God accomplished supernaturally at the resurrection of Christ. Please read Romans 6:1-11. If your life has been changed by this truth, then rejoice and praise the Lord as you read it. If this passage is new to you, or you don't understand it, please pray that the Lord will make it meaningful to you today.

According to Romans 6:1-11:
Who died?

Who was buried?

Who was raised from the dead?

What happened to sin and death?

And in my Southern accent, I ask you, "What do ya reckon happened to you?"

You have been healed from your terminal disease of sin, you have been released from the paralysis due to slavery and you have been given new life. Here's a message from the Great Physician: "Rise and walk!"

UNIT TEN
THE *Beautiful Bride*

LESSON ONE
THE HAND OF THE WISE
EPHESIANS 5:15-17

LESSON TWO
THE HARMONY OF THE SPIRIT
EPHESIANS 5:22-33

LESSON THREE
THE HEAD OF THE CHURCH
EPHESIANS 5:22-33

LESSON FOUR
THE HEAD OF THE HOME
EPHESIANS 5:22-33

LESSON ONE
THE *H*AND OF THE *W*ISE
EPHESIANS 5:15 — 17

Pray that you will learn to discern the opportunities which the Lord places before you to carry out His will.

There is a verse in our study today that always makes me a little nervous. Please read Ephesians 5:15-21 and then I'll tell you what it is!

Do any of the verses you just read make you "nervous," or apprehensive, confused or perhaps bring about some conviction? If so, I suggest you write a petition to the Lord here, mentioning the verses or phrases that concern you.

The phrase that concerns me may surprise you. I pray that the Lord will give me wisdom to understand how to "redeem the time." That phrase makes me nervous because it makes me think that I have to be busy, busy, busy. I'm looking forward to our study and trust that the Lord will clarify for us what He means by this phrase. Verses 18-21 as well as the rest of Chapters 5 and 6 will show us how to redeem the time and do the will of God.

Paul is still instructing the Ephesians on how to walk. My NKJV says to "walk circumspectly." But other versions say "be careful how you walk," and according to the scholars, that is a better translation. One other comment on this phrase says, "to walk circumspectly is to step gingerly. We should watch our path to avoid conflict with undesirable influences."[1] That makes a lot of sense in light of what we've been studying in Chapter 5.

Please look at Psalm 1:1 and make note of the same caution on how to walk.

I'm really eager to discover how to walk wisely, and not foolishly. Where do you turn for wisdom?

We studied wisdom in Ephesians 1, but once certainly isn't enough for such a topic. One of the verses that we looked at previously was 1 Corinthians 1:30 which says "of Him you are in Christ, who became for us wisdom from God."

Please look at James 3:13 and note how we are to behave wisely.

As I turn to the Lord for wisdom, He turns me to His Word in Proverbs. Please use your concordance and look up several verses from Proverbs that teach us about wisdom. Look up the word "wise" in a concordance and then look for the verses found in Proverbs. There are a total of 247 verses in the KJV of the Bible containing the word "wise"! There are at least 30 verses in Proverbs.

Try to find two verses that are meaningful to you.

You probably came across a few verses that contrasted the wise and the foolish. Look up the word "fool" or "foolish" in your concordance and please try to find two verses that explain the error of foolish ways.

Ephesians 5:15-17 give two very clear explanations of how to walk wisely. What are they?

I think the first explanation is dependent on the second. You can see an identical instruction from Paul in Colossians 4:5.

Look up the meaning for the following words, noting the aspect of the definitions that make sense for these two verses (Ephesians 5:15, Colossians 4:5).

Redeem – Strong's #1805
Greek word:
Greek definition:

Time – Strong's #2540
Greek word:
Greek definition:

> There are special favorable seasons for doing good, which occasionally present themselves, of which believers ought diligently to avail themselves. This constitutes true "wisdom". [2]

> Watch the time, and make it your own so as to control it; as merchants look out for opportunities, and accurately choose out the best goods; serve not the time, but command it, and it shall do what you approve. [3]

A wise person will make the right use of time, seizing on every opportunity to do good.

Think of a time recently where you walked wisely, redeemed the time and took the opportunity presented to you to do good. Note your reflections here.

I mentioned earlier that I think Paul's two specific instructions on how to walk carefully relate to each other. I need to understand what the Lord's will is in a situation so that I will redeem the time and seize the opportunities that He presents. This phrase indicates that we need to use our minds to discern the will of the Lord.

Please look up the meaning of the following words:
Understand – Strong's #4920
Greek word:
Greek definition:

Will – Strong's #2307
Greek word:
Greek definition:

Now look at the following references, recording what we are to understand and do.
Deuteronomy 4:5-6

John 7:17

Romans 12:2

What do you think Paul told the Ephesians to do to discover what the Lord's will was for them? Where did he point them to find the commands of the Lord? How did he teach them to renew their minds?

Where do you find the commands of the Lord, and with what do you renew your minds?

We live in the best time of all, and in the best country of all, regarding the availability of God's Word. We have so many translations and commentaries. Bibles are available everywhere. We are free to read, study and speak about God's Word. There are people-groups today that do not have the Word of God written in their language. There are countries today where Bibles are in short supply, yet in huge demand. Please cherish the Word of God and redeem the time that you have now. Things will not always be this way.

It is in the Word of God that we discover the clear, explicit will of the Lord. Please note His good and perfect will from the following verses.

1 Thessalonians 4:3

1 Thessalonians 5:18

1 Peter 2:15

You've just looked at the verses which expressly state "the will of God." But remember that all of Scripture, its instructions, commands and promises, communicate the will of God.

The following verses present you with a warning and a reward regarding doing the will of God. Praying Scripture will lead you to pray the will of God. Conclude today's lesson by turning the next two verses into prayers that you may be wise, redeem the time and understand the will of the Lord.

Luke 12:47

1 John 2:17

> Spend your time...
> in nothing which you know must be repented of;
> in nothing on which you might not pray for the blessing of God;
> in nothing which you could not review with a quiet conscience
> on your dying bed;
> in nothing which you might not safely and properly be found
> doing if death should surprise you in the act.[4]
> Richard Baxter (1615–1691)

THE *Harmony* OF THE *Spirit*

Pray that you will sense the presence of the Holy Spirit in your study today.

I hope that the Lord will teach us the next few verses in one sitting! Each phrase is worthy of individual analysis, but for our study, we will look at the big picture of Ephesians 5:18-21.

Begin reading Ephesians 5:15, continuing to verse 21. Paul is instructing the recipients of his letter to walk wisely and carefully.

What are the instructions in verses 18 through 21? (I found six.)

In the last lesson, one of our cross-references (1 Thessalonians 5:7) complemented and reinforced Paul's first instruction in Ephesians 3:18. In Chapter 4 and so far in Chapter 5, Paul teaches and instructs through many contrasts . . . Don't lie, speak truth. No corrupt words, but what is good. No foolish talking, but rather giving thanks. Once darkness, now light. Don't be foolish, but be wise. His instruction, "do not be drunk with wine" is not only a legitimate instruction to stop the bad habit of drunkenness, but it is a contrasting image to the concept of being filled with the Spirit. Don't be filled with wine, but be filled with the Spirit.

Drunkenness very frequently supplies biblical writers with striking metaphors and similes. It symbolizes intellectual or spiritual perplexity, bewilderment and helplessness under calamity. We see another contrast . . . understanding the will of the Lord (with a sound mind) versus spiritual perplexity and bewilderment.

Please note what you think the writers were trying to convey with their imagery of drunkenness in the following verses.

Job 12:25

Isaiah 19:14

Jeremiah 23:9

Ezekiel 23:32-34

Drunkenness is foolishness! Be filled with the Spirit! But aren't you already filled with the Spirit? You know that you are sealed with the Spirit. Hmmm. Does sealed mean that the Spirit is outside of you or inside of you? We looked at a verse while studying Chapter 1 that will clarify this for us — and leave no doubt!

Read 2 Corinthians 1:21-22. Where is the Holy Spirit?

Please look up the meaning for the following word.
Filled – Strong's #4137
Greek word:
Greek definition:

> God commands us to be filled with the Spirit, and if we are not filled, it is because we are living beneath our privileges.[5]
>
> Dwight Lyman Moody (1837–1899)

Turn back to the lesson "Filled with Fullness" on pages 95 and 96, and review the filling of the Spirit that we studied there. The book of Ephesians is filled with many mysteries, including the mystery of the Trinity! Who fills us?

And now back to Ephesians 5. Keep in mind the contrast which Paul has set up. The mental images of drunkenness are not a pretty sight, as we saw in the symbolism of the previous verses in the Old Testament. But the picture that Paul paints of those filled with the Spirit is beautiful.

What are the results, according to Ephesians 5:19-21 of being abundantly supplied and richly imparted with the Holy Spirit?

Please turn to Ephesians 5:1 and read this chapter through verse 21.

I know I've asked you to read and reread and reread this chapter! The Spirit moved through Paul to create a letter which is intricately woven together. Just a personal reflection here: Paul had so much to communicate, but he could only say it one word at a time. All of his teaching was connected however, whether by content, contrast or conclusion.

I think that Ephesians 5:19-21 stands in contrast specifically to verses 4, 6, 8-10 and 17. What do you think?

Psalms. Hymns. Spiritual songs. Singing. Making melody in your hearts. Does that all sound the same to you? Wouldn't you know it, using the incredible Greek language, Paul is not redundant! These are different words.

Please look each one up and note their definitions.
Psalms – Strong's #5568
Greek word:
Greek definition:

Hymns – Strong's #5215
Greek word:
Greek definition:

Songs – Strong's #5603
Greek word:
Greek definition:

Melody – Strong's #5567
Greek word:
Greek definition:

Please rewrite Ephesians 5:19 in your own words based on what you have just learned. You could even write it out as a new song if you are led to do so!

Are you ready to sing? I know there are some of you out there who do not like to open your mouth. Music may not inspire you, it may not touch you and it may not be a form of worship that you are comfortable with or enjoy. I'm not like that. I can't sing a solo, I'm not a songbird, but I make melodies in my heart. And I love music. A wide variety of music! Apparently, the Lord does too, and wants us to commune with Him and with each other in corporate worship.

Let's look at the following cross-references for a lesson in music appreciation. Our professor is the Holy Spirit. Describe what is happening in the following verses.

Exodus 15:1

1 Chronicles 15:16

Isaiah 30:29

Zephaniah 3:14-17

Matthew 26:30

1 Corinthians 14:15

James 5:13

Revelation 15:3

You will find one more exhortation regarding singing from Paul in Colossians 3:16-17. What is your response — to the Lord — to His desire for you to communicate with Him and His family in this way?

> The Holy Spirit is composer and conductor. He gives each member of the worshiping congregation sounds—which He weaves together in heavenly harmony.[6]

What would we do without the songs "Great Is Thy Faithfulness," "Holy, Holy, Holy," "Christ the Lord Is Risen Today" and "Joy to the World"? What would we do without "It Is Well With My Soul," and "Have Thine Own Way"? What would we do without "Jesus Loves Me"? The Lord has blessed many of His saints with amazing musical talent, whether it is composing, playing or singing. Give thanks for all things! (Ephesians 5:20) We will worship the Lamb that was slain with singing when we see Him. I think we will be singing new songs, but the "oldies" will remind us of the presence of the Spirit in us while we were on the earth.

THE 𝓗ead OF THE 𝓒hurch
EPHESIANS 5:22 — 33

Pray that you will comprehend the love of Christ for His bride.

Be filled with the Spirit . . . Speaking to one another in psalms . . . Making melody in your heart . . . Giving thanks always for all things . . . Submitting to one another in the fear of the Lord.

Have you experienced any times with other believers that included this type of fellowship? If so, please briefly describe one of them.

Paul doesn't skip a beat in his letter. He moves immediately from exhorting believers to submit to one another to specifically exhorting wives to submit to their husbands. We have come to an incredible, amazing, wonderful, mysterious passage of Scripture. Please anticipate knowing Jesus Christ in a deeper way as a result of studying these verses. Whether you are married or single, these verses hold precious truths and promises for us.

Please read Ephesians 5:22-33.

Let's keep our perspective straight here. Jesus Christ is the model for the husband. Much is explained to the Ephesians here about how Christ loves the church. We've observed throughout this letter that one of its major themes is oneness in the body of Christ, unity in the church.

Please begin your study of this Scripture by listing everything that you learn about Christ, including His relationship to the church, from Ephesians 5:22-33.

Just take a moment and think about this list of Christ's responsibilities regarding the church, the family of believers. What is your reaction to what Christ has done and is doing for His bride, the church?

Let's investigate some of the words used in our passage in Ephesians, and check out some cross-references as well. Please look up the meaning for the following word:

Head — Strong's #2776
Greek word:
Greek definition:

How was this word used in Ephesians 1:22-23 and Ephesians 4:15? See also Colossians 1:18.

Please look up the meaning for the following word:
Subject to – Strong's #5293
Greek word:
Greek definition:

The same Greek word is used in the following verses. Who is submitting to whom?
Luke 2:51

Luke 10:17

Romans 13:1

1 Peter 5:5

Please look up the meaning for the following words:
Loved – Strong's #25
Greek word:
Greek definition:

Gave – Strong's #3860
Greek word:
Greek definition:

How did Christ love the church? How did He give Himself for her? Look at the following verses for a reminder of this biblical truth.

Ephesians 5:2

Matthew 20:28

Luke 22:41-42

Ephesians 5:26-27 state that Christ gave Himself for the church so that He might sanctify and cleanse her, that He might present her to Himself as a glorious bride without any spot or wrinkle and that she would be perfectly holy without any blemish of any kind. This is a beautiful description of what the body of Christ, the bride of Christ, will be like one day. She will be perfect in beauty and splendidly adorned. One commentator said that she will be free from every indication of age, faultless and immortal.[7] Women everywhere would love to be loved in such a way that frees them from every indication of age!

How does Christ sanctify and cleanse His bride? With what does He wash her?

Look at the following verses and summarize your thoughts.
Ephesians 5:26

John 13:8-10

John 15:3

Psalm 119:9

Are you allowing Christ to wash you with His word and keep you clean each day? You probably have a daily routine regarding your personal hygiene. What is your daily routine regarding your personal sanctification?

The final aspect of Christ's love for the church that we are going to look at is described in Ephesians 5:29. Please look up the meaning for the following words:
Nourish – Strong's #1625
Greek word:
Greek definition:

Cherish – Strong's #2282
Greek word:
Greek definition:

From the Jamison, Fausset and Brown Commentary, I learned that these two words refer to the care that the husband regularly provides for his wife. To nourish refers to food and internal sustenance, while cherish refers to clothing and external fostering.[8]

How does Jesus nourish and cherish His bride? See John 6:51-56 and Matthew 6:25-33.

Jesus Christ is the only one who can perfect His bride. He has already done what no man can do — He paid the debt of our sin with His life. He rose from the dead. He appeared to many. He ascended into heaven. He sent His Holy Spirit. And now He continues His supernatural work. Only Jesus Christ can unify and sanctify millions of people and transform them into one beautiful bride for Himself.

L E S S O N   F O U R
THE *H*EAD OF THE *H*OME
E P H E S I A N S   5 : 2 2 — 3 3

You may have heard of the book "The Power of A Praying Wife" by Stormie Omartian. Please pray now for the power of the Holy Spirit so that we will be able to comprehend the role of the husband and wife which we are about to study.

Our society has come to the point where a biblical worldview is not the basis for the definition of marriage. So, to be clear on the individuals referred to as husband and wife, let me remind you that in the beginning: "God created man in His own image; in the image of God He created him; male and female He created them. Then God blessed them, and God said to them, 'Be fruitful and multiply'" Genesis 1:27-28 The Lord defined marriage as the union of one man and one woman.

Please read Ephesians 5:22-33 and list each specific responsibility given to husbands, as well as those implied responsibilities.

What is the main thing that the husband is to do?

Jesus Christ has commanded husbands to follow His example. Husbands have a high, holy and very heavy calling. Have you ever thought about that? What do you think about the responsibility that Christ has laid out before them?

Do you think there are any real-life, biblical examples of men loving their wives? Let's see . . .

Look at the following verses and describe how each man demonstrated his love for his wife.
Genesis 2:21-25

Genesis 29:18-19

1 Samuel 1:4-8

2 Samuel 12:24

Hosea 1:2-3; Hosea 3:1-3

Matthew 1:18-25

The verses you looked at represent just a few examples of the variety of ways that husbands may demonstrate their love to their wives. The lesson we are to learn from these verses is that Christ is the example for husbands, and they have a responsibility that is far greater than anything commanded to wives.

Keep that in mind as you now read Ephesians 5:22-33 for the specific instructions Paul gave to wives. Please list them below.

What are you thinking now? Who has the longer list of responsibilities? Who has the harder responsibility, the husband or the wife? What is your opinion regarding why the wife is to submit to the husband?

Earlier, I mentioned that this passage holds precious truths for us whether we are married or single. I want to emphasize that again. Whether you are married, single, divorced or widowed, the command given here by Paul to wives should be understood and respected. You may find yourself in a counseling or mentoring situation, or just in a conversation with a friend, and you should be prepared to advise according to God's Word.

Let's do our research on these specific instructions to wives.

Please look up the meaning for the following word:
Submit – Strong's #5293
Greek word:
Greek definition:

This word is also found in the following verses. Please make notes of what you learn in each verse.
Colossians 3:18

Titus 2:5

The King James Version of Ephesians 5:22 says, "Wives, submit *yourselves* to your own husbands, as unto the Lord." What difference does the addition of this word make to your understanding of the concept of the wife's submission to her husband?

Hupotasso, the Greek word that we are considering at the moment, has its origins in a military context. Its meaning emphasizes being under the authority of another. But surprisingly, it does not mean that one is forced to submit to authority. Instead, it means that one voluntarily places themselves under the proper authority of another. This leads us to interpret Paul's statement to wives as a command to voluntarily place themselves under the authority of their husbands.

As we continue our study of Paul's instructions regarding submitting to one another in the fear of the Lord (Ephesians 5:21), we will see a difference in the attitude and expectation of submission from children and servants. Paul will explain their subordination in terms of obedience, rather than voluntary submission.

There is a very important little word in the midst of this verse of other important words! To whom exactly are wives to submit?

Please consider the following notes from John MacArthur's Commentary on Ephesians, underlining that which is most meaningful to you.

Hupotasso means to relinquish one's rights, and the Greek middle voice (used in v.21 and carried over by implication into v.22) emphasizes the willing submitting of *oneself.* God's command is to those who are to submit. That is, the submission is to be a voluntary response to God's will in giving up one's independent rights to other believers in general and to ordained authority in particular—in this case the wife's **own husband.**

The wife is not commanded to obey (hupakouo) her husband, as children are to obey their parents and slaves their masters (6:1, 5). A husband is not to treat his wife as a servant or as a child, but as an equal for whom God has given him care and responsibility for provision and protection, to be exercised in love. She is not his to order about, responding to his every wish and command. As Paul proceeds to explain in considerable detail (vv. 25-33), the husband's primary responsibility as head of the household is to love, provide, protect, and serve his wife and family—not to lord it over them according to his personal whims and desires.

Your own husband suggests the intimacy and mutuality of the wife's submission. She willingly makes herself **subject to** the one she possesses as her **own husband** (cf. 1 Corinthians 7:3-4). [8]

I would like for you to undertake a contemplative exercise at this point. Please read Ephesians 5:22-33 again and look over your study notes on this passage so far, then consider and answer the following questions.

What is the *manner* of submission of wives described here?

What is the *motive* for submission of wives described here?

What is the *model* for submission of wives described here?

Please rejoice with me as we reflect on the ultimate model of submission — Jesus Christ Himself! We began our study into this passage yesterday observing that Christ is the model for the husband as the head of the family, but now we also see that He is all in all! He is also the perfect model of submission for wives. Isn't it amazing?!

There is much more that we could but will not study in this particular passage in Ephesians. Let's just observe that Paul quotes from Genesis 2:24, reminding us of God's original standard for marriage which has not changed even today. Two are to become one, and nothing is to separate them.

What is Paul's final instruction to the husband?

What is Paul's final instruction to the wife?

The husband is to agapaō his wife, and the wife is to phobeō her husband. The first word, agapaō is one that you looked up yesterday, meaning to love dearly and love with the desire for the very best for someone. This is the way that God loves us.

Please look up the meaning for "phobeō" which has been translated as respect or reverence in Ephesians 5:33.
Respect — Strong's # 5399
Greek word:
Greek definition:

*Phobeō is derived from **phobos** which is used in Ephesians 5:21: "and be subject to one another in the fear of the Lord." Some specifics of the grammar will add to our understanding of these words.*

The verb "love" in Ephesians 5:33 is in the present imperative active voice. This indicates a command to do something in the future which involves continuous or repeated action. The verb "respect" in this verse is in the present subjunctive middle/passive voice. The tense (present) refers to continuous or repeated action, regardless of when the action took place. The mood (subjunctive) suggests that the action is subject to some condition.

Nowhere in these verses does Paul mention a conditional word such as "if" or "therefore." He simply states that a wife is to submit to and respect her husband, whether he is godly or ungodly, believing or unbelieving, loving or unloving.

The point of all this grammatical information is that the Greek word for "respect" indicates that some condition must be in place for a wife to respect her husband. Nowhere does this passage indicate that a husband must be a Christian. The one condition or fact that is stated about the husband is that he is the head of the family. This is the "condition" which a wife must accept and then choose to respect her husband because he is the head of the family.

Now that you have the meanings of two key words in Paul's final exhortation to husbands and wives, please fill in the blanks below with your understanding of these two words.

Nevertheless let each one of you in particular so _____ his own wife

as himself, and let the wife see that she _____ her husband.

Do you see the magnitude of these instructions? Do you see that both the husband and the wife have a commission to do something that can only be accomplished by the Spirit of Christ moving through them? The husband is to love his wife dearly, completely, sacrificially, and unconditionally . . . as Christ loved each one of us! The wife is to revere, respect, honor and be in awe of her husband, recognizing his place of authority and responsibility.

For a look at the everyday life of the submissive, respectful wife, please turn to 1 Peter 3:1-6. What are the actions and attitudes of a devoted bride as described here?

To love, honor and cherish, till death do us part. Perhaps this is the hardest thing in the world for you to do right now. But this letter to the Ephesians is full of teachings of Christ in you, His power, His love, His Spirit. Let Him love through you.

For married women: Our final exercise will be one in which we either begin or continue to learn to submit to and respect our God-given husbands. Please pray that the Lord will provide a time for you to discuss this lesson with your husband. With respect and gentleness, approach your husband and ask him if there is any area in which you are not submitting to his leadership in your home. Ask him if he feels that you respect him. We will soon be looking at the very real spiritual warfare that goes on around us at all times. The home is a strategic battleground. Please take the time to strengthen your marriage according to the Word of the Lord.

For single, widowed, or divorced women: Thank you for walking through this study of the marriage relationship. I realize that it may have been difficult for you. I would like to ask you to continue to trust the Lord for what He is doing in your life, and please allow Him to be your Husband, your Beloved Bridegroom. Spend a few moments in communication with Him who is Head of *your* home.

FIGHTING FOR THE FAMILY

LESSON ONE
OBEDIENCE AND ADMONITION
EPHESIANS 6:1-4

LESSON TWO
RESPECT AND FAIRNESS
EPHESIANS 6:5-9

LESSON THREE
MAJESTY AND MALICE
EPHESIANS 6:10-13

LESSON FOUR
STRENGTH AND COURAGE
EPHESIANS 6:10-17

*O*BEDIENCE AND *A*DMONITION
E P H E S I A N S   6 : 1 — 4

Pray for the Holy Spirit to teach you all things today.

"I, therefore, the prisoner of the Lord, beseech you to walk worthy of the calling with which you were called, with all lowliness and gentleness, with longsuffering, bearing with one another in love, endeavoring to keep the unity of the Spirit in the bond of peace."

Do you know where that verse comes from? I hope that you recognize it as the first three verses from Ephesians 4, which began Paul's exhortation for daily conduct as a new creation in Christ. We have arrived at the last chapter of the letter to the Ephesians and Paul's teaching will stay strong until the end. Ephesians 6:1-9 continues with instructions to believers on submitting to one another in the fear of the Lord.

Please read Ephesians 5:15-21 for review, then read Ephesians 6:1-9.

What points from Ephesians 5:15-21 do you think should be kept in mind as we study Ephesians 6:1-9?

List each phrase from these two passages which refer to the Lord, God or Jesus Christ.

Based on these observations, what would you say is Paul's overriding message of motivation for individuals to behave in the way indicated?

I think we need to research the culture of family and social life in Ephesus during the time of the early church. Approximately what year was this letter written and received? What was the significance of the city of Ephesus? A study Bible or Bible dictionary should have this information in its introduction to Ephesians.

Children are a blessing from the Lord. But only the beautiful or strong ones. "Monstrous offspring we destroy; children too, if born feeble and ill-formed, we drown. It is not wrath, but reason, thus to separate the useless from the healthy." [1] "Exposure" of unwanted infants and children was the practice of Roman fathers during the early church period. At the father's command, a child would be taken to a desolate place and left to die in the elements, or be devoured by dogs and wild beasts. The father had absolute tyrannical authority over his children; he could sell his children just as he could any other propertty.

Consider this culture as you observe the commands given to children and fathers found in Ephesians 6:1-4. List the revolutionary words given to the Christian family.

It may be obvious to you that Paul is taking his instructions to children directly from the Ten Commandments. But remember to whom he was speaking. Gentiles. Previous pagans. Roman citizens whose culture placed higher value on their nation than their family.

Please look up the meaning for the following words:
Obey – Strong's #5219
Greek word:
Greek definition:

Honor – Strong's #5091
Greek word:
Greek definition:

In what setting do you think children heard Paul's personal admonition to them? It's just something to think about. Your speculations are admissible!

What reasons did Paul give the children for obeying their parents? You can share these reasons with children who you influence, too!

Times were hard for children. Yet, the Holy Spirit inspired Paul to teach them God's ways. The prophet Micah declared what he saw when the norms of society were broken down, saying: "For son dishonors father, daughter rises against her mother, daughter-in-law against her mother-in-law; a man's enemies are the men of his own household." (Micah 7:6).

Paul warned Timothy about the lawlessness of the last days. During this time there will be disobedience to parents (2 Timothy 3:1-2). The command to obey and honor is given to children, but the greater responsibility lies with the parents.

In one concise verse, Paul gives clear and weighty instruction to parents. Fill in the blanks below as we highlight their responsibilities.

And you, fathers, _____ _____ _____ your children to wrath, but _____ _____ _____ in the _____ and _____ of the Lord.

This instruction is given to "patēr" which has been translated fathers but can also indicate both parents. Given the cultural setting of the day, it is understandable that Paul would speak more directly to fathers regarding these instructions, but they do apply to both parents.

What actions or attitudes on the part of a parent normally provoke anger, irritation or resentment?

According to Colossians 3:21, what can happen when parents provoke their children?

I think the God-breathed words of Ephesians 6:4 probably left quite a few Ephesian fathers breathless! Not only were they not to provoke their children, they were to nurture, discipline, instruct and encourage them! The Roman Empire was stained with the blood of infants, but Christianity taught that children were valuable, their faith was exemplary, they would be joint-heirs of the kingdom of God, and they should be educated in religious and moral teachings.

Please look up the meaning for the following words.
Bring them up - Strong's#1625
Greek word:
Greek definition:

This same word is used in the Septuagint (the Greek version of the Old Testament) in Proverbs 23:24, but is often translated in English as "begets." How is the father described and what are the results of his nourishing?

Nurture - Strong's #3809
Greek word:
Greek definition:

This word is found in the Septuagint in Proverbs 3:11-12 and Proverbs 22:15. What insights do you gain into the reasons for and benefits of paideia?

Admonition - Strong's #3559
Greek word:
Greek definition:

I found that the Greek was translated in different ways in different versions of the Bible. How would you express the intended meaning of Ephesians 6:4 based on the definitions of the words above?

Peanut butter and jelly. Love and cherish. Father and son. Paideia and nouthesia. They each go together, one not being complete without the other. Perhaps you discovered in your own word dictionaries that nouthesia, admonition, means instruction mainly by word. And paideia, training, means instruction mainly by deed.

1 John 3:18 and Colossians 3:17 provide a good summary for this study of instruction to fathers. Consider these verses along with the rest of our study today. What was the radical new way that fathers were to carry out their responsibilities?

Close your study time today as an obedient child of God, honoring your Father in heaven.

Our Father, which art in heaven,
Hallowed be Thy Name.
Thy kingdom come.
Thy will be done in earth, as it is in heaven.
Give us this day our daily bread.
And forgive us our debts, as we forgive our debtors.
And lead us not into temptation,
But deliver us from evil:
For Thine is the kingdom, and the power, and the glory, forever. Amen.
Matthew 6:9-13 KJV

LESSON TWO
RESPECT AND FAIRNESS
EPHESIANS 6:5 — 9

Ask the Holy Spirit to show you what it means to be free.

In the previous lesson,, we considered the sad state of the Roman family during the time of the early church. The good news is that Jesus Christ has been making all things new since His resurrection. His truth, His life, and His Spirit have influenced the world in a way that nothing else could have. "The best legal enactments would never have been able to eradicate the evils of society without the spiritual influence of the church." [2] The evils of society included not only the insignificance of children, but also the inhumane treatment of men and women who were slaves.

It is essential to understand slavery as it existed in the first century. At that time, the slave-master relationship was as common as the employee-employer relationship is today.

Slavery in the Ancient World
During this period, the Jews practiced slavery according to the provisions of the Law of Moses. A Jewish slave belonged to the family of the owner and had certain religious and social rights. If the slave was a Hebrew, the term of slavery was limited to six years. Jeremiah had warned that permanent slavery would bring about divine disfavor (Jer. 34:8–22). But even if the slave was a Gentile, the owner's power was limited by Jewish law. If a master punished and injured a slave in his possession, the slave was to be set free. If the punishment resulted in the slave's death, then the master was to be punished. The slave was viewed as a person and was to be treated fairly, which differed from the Roman system of slavery.

Among the Jews, slaves were only a small part of the total population. But in Rome, slaves outnumbered Roman citizens. Some of the wealthy Roman landowners may have had ten to twenty thousand slaves working on their estates. To the Romans, a slave was not a person and was basically thought of as property. Though many slaves were treated humanely and sometimes were better off economically than many free persons, there was still the fact that they were considered a possession. They were vulnerable to cruel treatment and could even be killed with impunity. With slaves far outnumbering citizens, controlling the slave population was an imperative to the Romans. To lose control of the slaves was to forfeit the social and economic basis of the Roman Empire.[3]

The history of the United States includes the Civil War which was fought because of economical as well as societal issues. Slavery was as horrible in the 1800s as it was in the 100s. Just thinking about the atrocious, cruel, merciless treatment of individuals, made in the image of God, brings me to tears. The apostle Paul must have grieved over what he observed as he traveled throughout the Roman territories.

With this in mind, please read what Paul said to slaves and masters in Ephesians 6:5-9. What are his instructions, and which, if any, surprise you?

In what setting do you think the slaves and masters would have heard these exhortations?

These verses include several contrasts. Please record them below.

Quoted below is the KJV of Ephesians 6:5-9, with Strong's Concordance numbers included.[4] First, highlight, circle or underline the repeated words "servants" and "masters" - those that have the identical Strong's numbers. Some of the words are identical in the Greek, but have been translated as different words in the English.

6:5   Servants,[1401] be obedient[5219] to them that are *your* masters[2962] according[2596] to the flesh,[4561] with[3326] fear[5401] and[2532] trembling,[5156] in[1722] singleness[572] of your[5216] heart,[2588] as[5613] unto Christ;[5547]

6:6   Not[3361] with[2596] eyeservice,[3787] as[5613] menpleasers;[441] but[235] as[5613] the servants[1401] of Christ,[5547] doing[4160] the[3588] will[2307] of God[2316] from[1537] the heart;[5590]

6:7   With[3326] goodwill[2133] doing service,[1398] as[5613] to the[3588] Lord,[2962] and[2532] not[3756] to men:[444]

6:8   Knowing[1492] that[3754] whatsoever[3739, 5100, 1437] good thing[18] any man[1538] doeth,[4160] the same[5124] shall he receive[2865] of[3844] the[3588] Lord,[2962] whether[1535] *he be* bond[1401] or[1535] free.[1658]

6:9   And,[2532] ye masters,[2962] do[4160] the[3588] same things[846] unto[4314] them,[846] forbearing[447] threatening:[547] knowing[1492] that[3754] your[5216] Master[2962] also[2532] is[2076] in[1722] heaven;[3772] neither[2532, 3756] is[2076] there respect of persons[4382] with[3844] Him.[846] KJV

Did you find #1401 three times, and #2962 five times?

Now please look up the meaning of the following words found in the passage above:
Servants – Strong's #1401
Greek word:
Greek definition:

Obedient – Strong's #5219
Greek word:
Greek definition:

Masters – Strong's #2962
Greek word:
Greek definition:

Singleness – Strong's #572
Greek word:
Greek definition:

Eyeservice – Strong's #3787
Greek word:
Greek definition:

Men-pleasers – Strong's #441
Greek word:
Greek definition:

Service – Strong's #1398
Greek word:
Greek definition:

Free – Strong's #1658
Greek word:
Greek definition:

What insights do you have on instructions to slaves based on these definitions?

Gill's Commentary explains that Paul repeatedly mentioned the duty of servants in his letters because, "generally speaking, they [servants] were more rude and ignorant, and less pains were taken with them to instruct them; they were apt to be impatient and weary of the yoke; and scandal was like to arise from servants in the first ages of Christianity through some libertines, and the licentiousness of the false teachers, who insinuated, that servitude was inconsistent with Christian freedom." [5]

Is servitude inconsistent with Christian freedom? Please look at the following references and note what you learn.

1 Corinthians 7:22

1 Corinthians 12:13

Galatians 3:28

Colossians 3:11

Ephesians 6:5-9 is clearly about the relationship between a master and a slave, and the attitude that one should have to another. The apostle Paul did not approve of or condone slavery, but neither did he condemn it or set about on a crusade to abolish it. Instead, he exhorted Christian slaves to demonstrate submission, obedience and humility to their masters whether they were believers or not. Paul also exhorted Christian masters to behave in a way that was different from the cultural norm and treat their slaves fairly.

As I mentioned earlier in the lesson, Jesus Christ has influenced the world in a way that no one else could have. As Paul taught the equality in Christ of both slaves and free persons, he declared a principle that would eventually undermine the institution of slavery as it existed at that time.

I would like to return to an earlier question: Is servitude inconsistent with Christian freedom? The short answer is no. In fact, the cross of Christ set us free so that we can serve.

Please read Romans 6:15-22. Please write the verse from this passage that explains most clearly to you our freedom to be bondservants.

Whether you are a slave to the stove or the office telephone, whether you are a slave to a CEO or the "A, B, Cs" (homework!), whether you are a slave to the computer or the carpool line, in each case, you are to live under the Emancipation Proclamation issued by Almighty God and the Lord Jesus Christ. You are free! Free indeed, to do the will of God from your heart, as to Him and not as to men.

Who is your Master? What instructions has He given to you, His bondservant today? The lesson to the slaves and masters was ultimately to touch their hearts. How does it touch yours?

> If a man does only what is required of him, he is a slave.
>
> If a man does more than is required of him, he is a free man.[6]
> Chinese Proverb

LESSON THREE

$\mathcal{M}$AJESTY AND $\mathcal{M}$ALICE

EPHESIANS 6:10 — 13

Spend a few moments in adoration of the Lord God Omnipotent, who reigns on high.

Finally. Finally? Finally! We have arrived at the last major exhortation from Paul to the Ephesians. He will conclude his letter with a gracious greeting, but before he does that, he's going to recruit the believers to be soldiers in the army of the Lord! There is a war going on, and the final battle is still in the future. Until the Day of the Lord, all believers need to be ready to fight.

Please read Ephesians 6:10-18 aloud.

There are many different ways that we could approach our study of this passage. I'm excited to begin with a look at the Lord's position as Commander-in-Chief!

Please look at the following verses and note where He resides.
Psalm 11:4

Revelation 4:2,5:13

Now look at Isaiah 14:12-14 and note what you discover in this verse. What does it tell you about Satan and what does he want?

Paul mentions the heavens quite often in his letter to the Ephesians. Please look up the Greek definitions to the following words and then note how it is used in the verses given.
Heavenly — Strong's #2032
Greek word:
Greek definition:

Ephesians 1:3

Ephesians 1:20

Ephesians 2:6

Ephesians 3:10

Ephesians 6:12

Heaven(s) - Strong's #3772
Greek word:
Greek definition:

Ephesians 1:10

Ephesians 3:15

Ephesians 4:10

Ephesians 6:9

Consider the truths that you've looked at thus far in the lesson. Are they encouraging or discouraging? Why?

Once again, please read Ephesians 6:10-18.

Why does Paul tell the Ephesians to be strong in the Lord? Answer, as specifically as you can, using words and phrases from the text.

In Ephesians 6:10-18 below, please mark every reference to the devil, including words and phrases which indicate his evil acts and intentions.

[10]Finally, my brethren, be strong in the Lord and in the power of His might. [11]Put on the whole armor of God, that you may be able to stand against the wiles of the devil. [12]For we do not wrestle against flesh and blood, but against principalities, against powers, against the rulers of the darkness of this age, against spiritual hosts of wickedness in the heavenly places. [13]Therefore take up the whole armor of God, that you may be able to withstand in the evil day, and having done all, to stand. [14]Stand therefore, having girded your waist with truth, having put on the breastplate of righteousness, [15]and having shod your feet with the preparation of the gospel of peace; [16]above all, taking the shield of faith with which you will be able to quench all the fiery darts of the wicked one. [17]And take the helmet of salvation, and the sword of the Spirit, which is the Word of God; [18]praying always with all prayer and supplication in the Spirit, being watchful to this end with all perseverance and supplication for all the saints.

Look up the meaning for the following words and note how it is used in the verses given.
Principalities — Strong's #746
Greek word:
Greek definition:

Ephesians 1:21

Ephesians 3:10

Ephesians 6:12

Power — Strong's #1849
Greek word:
Greek definition:

Ephesians 1:21

Ephesians 2:2

Ephesians 3:10

Ephesians 6:12

Ephesians 6:12 refers to the "rulers of the darkness of this age." Each reference to evil in this verse is plural. The devil has many enslaved to his hateful schemes. Look up the meaning for the following word and note what you learn from the verses given.

Prince — Strong's #758
Greek word:
Greek definition:

Ephesians 2:2

Matthew 12:24

John 12:31

John 14:30

As we enlist in the army of the Lord as the Ephesians did, we can know that we are joining a conquering King. Please look at Colossians 2:13-15 and note the victory already accomplished by the Lord Jesus Christ.

The end has not yet come, when Christ will deliver the kingdom to God and when He will put an end to all rule and all authority and power. He must reign till He has put all His enemies under His feet; the last enemy to be destroyed is death. (1 Corinthians 15:24-26) Until the end, God allows Satan to rule as the prince of the power of the air. There is a real war going on, and in tomorrow's lesson we will take up the armor with which we will be able to stand firm against the enemy. Thanks be to God who always leads us in triumph in Christ! (2 Corinthians 2:14)

I want you to end today's lesson with complete assurance from God's Word that you are safe in the embrace of the Almighty.

Turn to Romans 8:38-39 and personalize this verse as a statement of your belief and your prayer.

> Safe in Jehovah's keeping,
> Safe in temptation's hour.
> Safe in the midst of perils,
> Kept by Almighty power.
> Safe when the tempest rages,
> Safe though the night be long;
> E'en when my sky is darkest
> God is my strength and song.[7]
> Sir Robert Anderson (1841–1918)

LESSON FOUR

STRENGTH AND COURAGE
EPHESIANS 6:10 — 17

Our help comes from the Lord, Who made heaven and earth. Call out to Him today.

Be strong! Suit up! Stand firm! And pray always. In the last lesson, we looked into the heavenlies and saw that there is an evil one who wants to be seated on the throne of God. The throne is already occupied by the Creator of the Universe, the Sovereign King of Kings, the Lamb that was slain.

Paul tells the Ephesians to:

"put on the whole armor of God, that you may be able to stand against the

_____ of the devil."

This is the Greek word, methodeia, Strong's #3180. Zhodiates Word Study dictionary defines it this way: "to work by method; the following or pursuing of an orderly and technical procedure in the handling of a subject. In the New Testament, connected with evil doing."[8] This word could also be translated as cunning arts, deceit, craft, schemes or trickery. This is the method of the Lord's enemy. What is the enemy's mission?

Look at the following verses and describe Satan's objectives.

Luke 22:31

John 10:10

2 Corinthians 11:3

Revelation 12:10

As you observed in Luke 22:31, Peter had a close encounter with the devil. He experienced his wicked methods and schemes, but was not destroyed by them because Christ had prayed for him. Peter's familiarity with Satan gave him wisdom with which to counsel the early church. His admonition goes hand in hand with Paul's exhortation.

What does Peter say in 1 Peter 5:8-9?

Now we will return to Ephesians 6:10-18. Please list the actions that believers are to take so that they may be able to stand against the evil one. Use the words and phrases that you find in the Scriptures.

Do you see any command given to march, attack or advance on the enemy? What is the position that the soldier of the Lord is to have?

We could do a study in and of itself on the word "stand." It is used throughout the whole Bible, often in the context of a battle. The Lord gave the nation of Israel many victories, such that other nations knew that they could not stand against them. Other nations could not defeat the Israelites. But when the Israelites disobeyed the Lord, they could not stand against their enemies.

What can you learn from this and apply to yourself as you plan to stand against spiritual wickedness in high places?

Look at Exodus 14:13 for the attitude and expectation that we can have when we are strong in the Lord and in the power of His might. Note what you learn.

How can we "fear not" when we are standing face to face with a roaring lion, a great dragon, that old serpent, the accuser of the brethren? First, we can fear not because we know who reigns from the throne of heaven, as we studied yesterday. Second, we fear not because we have resurrection power residing in us through the Holy Spirit, as we have learned in previous lessons. Third, we fear not because we are outfitted in exclusive armor — produced and provided by Lord Sabaoth.

Let's consider the various equipment that we wear as we stand firm. Fill in the blanks of the following phrases from Scripture.

Waist girded with _____

Breastplate of _____

Feet shod with _____ ___ _____

Shield of _____

Helmet of _____

_____ **of the Spirit which is the** _____ **of God**

Fear knocked at the door. Faith answered. No one was there.[9]

—Inscription at Hind's Head Inn, Bray, England

While Paul explained this protective gear in the language of a Roman soldier's armor, he did not create the pieces of armor himself. Paul certainly was familiar with Isaiah's prophesies of the Messiah.

Look at the following references in which you will find that almost every piece of armor in Ephesians is mentioned. Note what you observe.

Isaiah 11:5

Isaiah 49:2

Isaiah 52 : 7

Isaiah 59:17

We learned early on in Ephesians that we are in Christ, and He is in us. If Christ is clothed with the armor as described in Isaiah, what does that mean for us?

It won't surprise you to learn that Paul exhorted churches through other letters to stand firm in the strength of the Lord. How are believers to stand, according to the following verses?
Romans 5:2

1 Corinthians 16:13

2 Corinthians 6:7

Galatians 5:1

What very important truth do you learn from Psalm 111:8 and Isaiah 40:8?

What has impacted you the most from today's study?

*We **stand still** in anticipation, we **stand by** in readiness, we **stand up** in strength, we **stand for** the Lord, we **stand out** because of righteousness. And the devil **doesn't stand a chance** — against Jesus Christ, Faithful and True, alive in you.*

We have one more week of study together! Stand strong and tall till the end!

UNIT TWELVE
The *Whole Truth*

LESSON ONE
STANDING ON THE PROMISES
EPHESIANS 6:14-17

LESSON TWO
REMEMBERING THE PROMISES
EPHESIANS 6:18-20

LESSON THREE
TREASURING THE PROMISES
EPHESIANS 6:21-24

LESSON FOUR
BELIEVING THE PROMISES
EPHESIANS 1:1-6:24

LESSON ONE
STANDING ON THE PROMISES
EPHESIANS 6:14—17

> Standing on the promises that cannot fail,
>
> When the howling storms of doubt assail,
>
> By the living Word of God I shall prevail,
>
> Standing on the promises of God.[1]

Pray that the promises of God will enable you to stand firm.

Do you remember where Paul was standing when he wrote the Ephesians? He knew that he was standing before the Lord of Hosts! He was also standing in prison in Rome and was well-acquainted with the guards. Imprisoning Paul didn't make him a captive; it only gave him an opportunity to preach to a captive audience — those in cells near him and those in the halls guarding him!

Throughout his letter to the Ephesians, Paul spoke to them in their language, using illustrations with which they would be familiar. As he shares his final thoughts, he continues to do so. The citizens of Ephesus were very aware of the Roman military. The Ephesians were also familiar with the idea of their gods giving armor to mythical heroes.

Look at Ephesians 6:11 and 13. What does Paul repeat here? How many pieces of armor is the believer to put on? Why do you think this is emphasized?

Think of each piece of armor and describe what part of your body as well as your soul it protects.

Using commentaries, word study dictionaries or Bible dictionaries, see what you can learn about the various pieces of armor listed in Ephesians 6:14-17.

The one offensive weapon named by Paul is the sword of the Spirit, which is the Word of God. Please look up the meaning of the following word:

Word — Strong's #4487 (see also root word, #4483)
Greek word:
Greek definition:

How does Hebrews 4:12 describe the Word of God?

After declaring the Word of God as the weapon to carry as we wear the full armor, Paul immediately commands a specific action. What is it?

We can look at the model of Jesus' warfare with the enemy in the wilderness for a better understanding of standing firm with the Word of God and prayer.

Please read Matthew 4:1-11, with the understanding that fasting was a method of prayer. How did Jesus respond to Satan's schemes?

Please read 2 Corinthians 10:3-6. What correlations do you see in these verses with the temptation of Christ? How do these verses describe the weapons of believers, the sword and prayer? What is the aggressive action that the soldier of the Lord must take?

> Occupy your mind with good thoughts, or the enemy will fill it with bad ones: unoccupied it cannot be.[2]
> Sir Thomas More (1478–1535)

Jesus wielded the sword of the Spirit against the lies of the devil, speaking the specific rhema of Scripture. You don't just carry the Bible as your sword; you carry the individual truths of the Bible as your sword. As a soldier of the Lord, standing firm in battle, you must know the creed. You must know what you believe. In this study on Ephesians, you've written a declaration of who you are in Christ, and who you are as a new creation.

Please write one more personal statement: a declaration of your doctrinal beliefs. Complete the phrases on the next page. Give at least one Scripture reference for each statement.

I believe that God_____

_____

I believe that Jesus_____

_____

I believe that the Holy Spirit_____

_____

I believe that heaven_____

_____

I believe that hell_____

_____

ℛEMEMBERING THE ℱROMISES

But the end of all things is at hand: be ye therefore sober, and watch unto prayer. 1 Peter 4:7

Even though Paul was many miles away, he enlisted the Ephesians as soldiers to fight on behalf of other believers as well as on his behalf when he requested their prayers. What were his specific requests?

Look at the following references to prayer and note for whom or what the prayers are being offered or requested.

Luke 6:28

Luke 10:2

2 Corinthians 5:20

2 Thessalonians 3:1

1 Timothy 2:1-4

James 5:16

Please summarize what you learn about how to pray for others from these examples.

Do you have any particular burden from the Lord to intercede on behalf of any person, any people groups, any situations or any ministries?

Do you have a plan for carrying out your ministry of intercession?

Consider the placement of the word, *watchful,* in the midst of Ephesians 6:18. Look at the verse below, fill in the blank, and then underline the words "prayer" and "supplication." Circle the words which describe how to pray, and draw lines connecting them to the underlined words.

. . . Praying always with all prayer and supplication in the Spirit, being

_____ to this end will all perseverance and supplication for all the saints...

What do you learn from this exercise?

Please look up the meaning for the following word:
Watchful — Strong's #69
Greek word:
Greek definition:

Why do you think Paul used this word in his exhortation to pray?

Paul uses several words in Ephesians 6:18-20 that reflect much of what he has shared through his letter to the Ephesians. What comes to mind from our studies with the following words?

    Spirit

    All the saints

    Mystery

I love it that even after all that Paul has taught, explained, exhorted, and demonstrated through his own life, he still wants to make known "the mystery of the gospel."

How and where does he want to make it known?

Please look up the meaning for the following word:
Ambassador — Strong's #4243
Greek word:
Greek definition:

How does this word relate to what we learned in Ephesians 1:3-5, 2:6, 2:13 and 2:19?

Make this personal. Write out a formal statement from the Lord commissioning you to be His royal ambassador.

Congratulations! You are not only a soldier, but a fully commissioned ambassador! The Lord has many plans for you!

L E S S O N   T H R E E
*T*REASURING THE *P*ROMISES
E P H E S I A N S   6 : 2 1 — 2 4

Pray that the Holy Spirit will continue to teach you through the Word of God.

We have come to the end of the letter. Paul's dear friends in Ephesus wept when he left them a few years before, and they were probably sad once again to see the last paragraph in this message to them. I expect they would have enjoyed hearing more from their beloved pastor.

Turn back to Ephesians 3:8-13, read this passage and then continue with Ephesians 6:21-24.

Based on these two passages, what did Paul want for the Ephesians?

What touches you the most from these two passages as you eavesdrop on his personal communication with his brethren?

Ephesians 6:21-22 teach us an important lesson regarding the church, unity and support. Why did Paul send Tychius to Ephesus?

Paul didn't isolate himself from other believers even when the Romans had tried to separate him from everyone else. Paul shared his concerns and needs and how he was doing with his fellow believers. He wasn't too good or too strong or too independent to receive prayer from his flock.

What role do you have that this could apply to in your life? Or who do you know that is in ministry that you can encourage?

We've come to the last words to the Ephesians now. Paul gives a summary of the gospel with four key words in these closing sentences of Ephesians 6:23-24. What are these four words?

Shalom. Peace.
This was the traditional greeting in the Jewish world. The Ephesians were no longer Gentiles after the flesh, but one in Christ, fellow citizens with the saints and members of the household of God.
Review Paul's message of peace given in the following verses of Ephesians:

Ephesians 1:2, 2:14-15, 2:17, 4:3, 6:15, 6:23

Choose and write out one of these verses on peace to keep as a precious gem mined from the riches of this book of Scripture.

Agape. Love.
The Ephesians now knew the width and length and depth and height of the love of God as well as the witness they would have to their world when they walked in love.

Review Paul's message of love given in the following verses of Ephesians:
Ephesians 1:4, 1:15, 2:4, 3:17, 3:19, 4:2, 4:15-16, 5:2,5:25, 5:28, 5:33, 6:23-24

Choose and write out one of these verses on love to keep as another precious gem found in the depths of this Scripture.

Pistis. Faith.
These believers were saved through faith and shared unity in faith and could stand firm with the shield of faith.

Review Paul's message of faith given in the following verses of Ephesians:
Ephesians 1:15, 2:8, 3:12, 3:17, 4:5, 4:13, 6:16, 6:23

Choose and write out one of these verses on faith to keep as a precious gem mounted on your shield.

Charis. Grace.
From beginning to end — grace. To the praise of the glory of His — grace. Redemption and forgiveness, from the riches of His — grace. His incredible gift — grace.

Review Paul's message of grace given in the following verses of Ephesians:
Ephesians 1:2, 1:6-7, 2:5, 2:7-8,3:2, 3:7-8, 4:7, 4:29, 6:24.

Choose and write out one of these verses on grace as a precious gem, given to you from the richest King ever known in eternity past, present or future.

> The Lord pour out His Spirit upon us that every chamber of our nature
>> may be sweetened and perfumed with the indwelling of God,
>> till our imagination shall only delight in things chaste and pure;
>> till our memory shall cast our the vile stuff from the dark chambers;
>> till we shall expect and long for heavenly things,
>> and our treasure shall all be in heaven and our heart be there.[3]
>> Charles Spurgeon

ℬELIEVING THE ℱROMISES

E P H E S I A N S   1 : 1 — 6 : 2 4

Our time together is complete. But, please, oh please, do not let my words in print be the last words that you read regarding Ephesians. Please return to the Written Word, through which you meet with the Living Word, and read the letter to the Ephesians from beginning to end once more. **Believe** *these divinely inspired promises and* **live** *what you* **believe.** *Let the last words of this study be between you and the One who is able to do immeasurably more than all we ask or imagine, according to His power that is at work within us. To Him be glory in the church and in Christ Jesus throughout all generations, for ever and ever! Amen.*

Just between me and Thee, My Lord . . .
My reflections on how You have blessed me ***immeasurably more***
than I could ever have imagined:

ENDNOTES

Unit One—From Sinners to Saints
1. Edythe Draper, *Draper's Quotations for the Christian World*, Tyndale House Publishers, Inc. Wheaton, Illinois.
2. Draper, *Draper's Quotations*
3. Draper, *Draper's Quotations*
4. Draper, *Draper's Quotations*

Unit Two—Just Like Jesus
1. From *The Nelson Study Bible*, copyright © 1997 by Thomas Nelson, Inc. Used by permission.
2. Draper, *Draper's Quotations*
3. Draper, *Draper's Quotations*
4. From *The Nelson Study Bible*, copyright © 1997 by Thomas Nelson, Inc. Used by permission.
5. Reuben Morgan, "So Blessed", © 1999 Reuben Morgan, Hillsong Publishing
6. From *The Nelson Study Bible*, copyright © 1997 by Thomas Nelson, Inc. Used by permission.
7. Kenneth Boa, *Face to Face: Praying the Scriptures for Intimate Worship*, Zondervan Publishing House, Grand Rapids, Michigan

Unit Three—Extravagant Prayer and Power
1. A. W. Tozer, *The Knowledge of the Holy*, HarperCollins Publishers, New York
2. Draper, *Draper's Quotations*
3. Draper, *Draper's Quotations*

Unit Four—All About Grace
1. Draper, *Draper's Quotations*
2. John Gill, *John Gill's Exposition of the Entire Bible,* www.e-sword.net
3. "Amazing Grace". Public Domain
4. Charles Spurgeon, *All of Grace*
5. Draper, *Draper's Quotations*
6. M. G. Easton, *Easton's Bible Dictionary*, www.e-sword.net
7. Draper, *Draper's Quotations*

Unit Five—The Presence of the Lord
1. John W. Thompson and Randy Scruggs, "Sanctuary", © 1982 Whole Armor Music, Full Armor Publishing
2. Draper, *Draper's Quotations*
3. Draper, *Draper's Quotations*
4. Draper, *Draper's Quotations*

Unit Six—The Power of His Love
1. Lewis E. Jones, "There is Power in the Blood", 1899
2. Draper, *Draper's Quotations*
3. Lawrence O. Richards, *The Bible Reader's Companion*, Victor Books, Scripture Press Publications, Inc. USA, Canada, England
4. Richards, *The Bible Reader's Companion*
5. "Jesus Loves Me", Public Domain

Unit Seven—Living the Abundant Life
1. J.H. Thayer, *Thayer's Greek Definitions*, www.e-sword.net
2. Draper, *Draper's Quotations*
3. Thayer, *Thayer's Greek Definitions*
4. Draper, *Draper's Quotations*

Unit Eight—Growing up Together
1. Marvin Vincent, *Vincent's Word Studies*, www.e-sword.net
2. Charles Hodge, *Ephesians*, Crossway Books, Good News Publishers, Wheaton, Illinois
3. Draper, *Draper's Quotations*

Unit Nine—Know by Our Love
1. Draper, *Draper's Quotations*
2. Draper, *Draper's Quotations*
3. *International Standard Bible Encyclopedia*, ed. James Orr, www.e-sword.net
4. *International Standard Bible Encyclopedia*
5. Gill, *Gill's Exposition*
6. *Jamieson, Fausset and Brown Commentary*, www.e-sword.net
7. Richards, *The Bible Reader's Companion*
8. *International Standard Bible Encyclopedia*
9. Gill, *Gill's Exposition*
10. *International Standard Bible Encyclopedia*
11. Vincent, *Vincent's Word Studies*
12. Vincent, *Vincent's Word Studies*
13. *Holman Bible Dictionary*, ed. Trent C. Butler, Ph.D.
14. Alfred Edersham, *The Life and Times of Jesus the Messiah*
15. Matthew Henry, *Matthew Henry's Consice Commentary*, www.e-sword.net

Unit Ten—The Beautiful Bride
1. From *The Nelson Study Bible*, copyright © 1997 by Thomas Nelson, Inc. Used by permission.
2. *Jamieson, Fausset and Brown Commentary*
3. *Jamieson, Fausset and Brown Commentary*
4. Draper, *Draper's Quotations*
5. Draper, *Draper's Quotations*
6. Draper, *Draper's Quotations*
7. Charles Hodge, *Ephesians*, Crossway Books, Good News Publishers, Wheaton, Illinois
8. *Jamieson, Fausset and Brown Commentary*
9. John MacArthur, 1996, c1986. *Ephesians*. Moody Press: Chicago

Unit Eleven—Fighting for the Family
1. Philip Schaff, *History of the Christian Church*
2. Philip Schaff, *History of the Christian Church*
3. From *The Nelson Study Bible*, copyright © 1997 by Thomas Nelson, Inc. Used by permission.
4. *King James Version plus Strong's Concordance Numbers*, www.e-sword.net
5. Gill, *Gill's Exposition*
6. Draper, *Draper's Quotations*
7. Draper, *Draper's Quotations*
8. *The Complete Word Study Dictionary*, ed. Spiros Zhodiates, AMG Publishers, Chattanooga, TN
9. Draper, *Draper's Quotations*

Unit Twelve—The Whole Truth
1. "Standing on the Promises", Public Domain
2. Draper, *Draper's Quotations*
3. Draper, *Draper's Quotations*

Suggested Resources

The Complete Word Study Dictionary, New Testament, Spiros Zhodiates
The Strongest Strong's Exhaustive Concordance by James Strong — available through online resources below and Google

Suggested (free) online study helps:
These include various Bible translations and links to all resources mentioned below.

studylight.org   **searchgodsword.org**   **blueletterbible.org**

e-sword.net (free program to download, then available offline)

The following list includes study helps that are available for free online if you are interested in pursuing more information about the Scriptures on your own. Descriptions are from e-sword.net.

Commentaries:
Robertson's Word Pictures in the New Testament
Robertson's magnum opus has a reputation as one of the best New Testament word study sets. Providing verse-by-verse commentary, it stresses meaningful and pictorial nuances implicit in the Greek but often lost in translation. And for those who do not know Greek, exegetical material and interpretive insights are directly connected with studies in the original text. All Greek words are transliterated.

Treasury of Scriptural Knowledge
This classic Bible study help gives you a concordance, chain-reference system, topical Bible and commentary all in one! Turn to any Bible passage, and you'll find chapter synopses, key word cross-references, topical references, parallel passages and illustrative notes that show how the Bible comments on itself. This really is a treasure!

Vincent's Word Studies
Marvin Vincent's Word Studies has been treasured by generations of pastors and laypeople. Commenting on the meaning, derivation, and uses of significant Greek words and idioms, Vincent helps you incorporate the riches of the New Testament in your sermons or personal study without spending hours on tedious language work!

John Gill's Exposition of the Entire Bible
Having preached in the same church as C. H. Spurgeon, John Gill is little known, but his works contain gems of information found nowhere outside of the ancient Jewish writings. John Gill presents a verse-by-verse exposition of the entire Bible.

Jamieson, Fausset and Brown Commentary

Long considered one of the best conservative commentaries on the entire Bible, the JFB Bible Commentary offers practical insight from a reformed evangelical perspective. The comments are an insightful balance between learning and devotion, with an emphasis on allowing the text to speak for itself.

Keil & Delitzsch Commentary on the Old Testament

This commentary is a classic in conservative biblical scholarship! Beginning with the nature and format of the Old Testament, this evangelical commentary examines historical and literary aspects of the text, as well as grammatical and philological issues. Hebrew words and grammar are used, but usually in content, so you can follow the train of thought.

Matthew Henry's Concise Commentary

Get the best of Matthew Henry — from his acclaimed writings to his insightful study outlines. Matthew Henry's warm mix of scholarship and practical application has made his commentary a favorite of preachers and devotional readers alike.

Dictionaries:

Easton's Bible Dictionary

Easton's Bible Dictionary provides informative explanations of histories, people and customs of the Bible. An excellent and readily understandable source of information for the student and layperson. This dictionary is one of Matthew George Easton's most significant literary achievements.

International Standard Bible Encyclopedia

This authoritative reference dictionary explains every significant word in the Bible and Apocrypha! Learn about archaeological discoveries, the language and literature of Bible lands, customs, family life, occupations, and the historical and religious environments of Bible people.

Smith's Bible Dictionary

A classic reference, this comprehensive Bible dictionary gives you thousands of easy-to-understand definitions, verse references and provides a wealth of basic background information that you'll find indispensable as you read the Bible.

Thayer's Greek Definitions

For over a century, Joseph Henry Thayer's Greek-English Lexicon of the New Testament has been lauded as one of the finest available! Based on the acclaimed German lexicon by C.L.W. Grimm, Thayer's work adds comprehensive extra-biblical citations and etymological information, expanded references to other works, increased analysis of textual variations, and discussion of New Testament synonyms. An invaluable resource for students of New Testament Greek!

PRAYER REQUESTS AND PRAISES
TODAY'S DATE:

My personal request:

Confidential requests from my friends:

Do not be anxious about anything, but in everything, by prayer and petition,
with thanksgiving, present your requests to God.
Philippians 4:6 NIV

PRAYER REQUESTS AND PRAISES
TODAY'S DATE:

My personal request:

Confidential requests from my friends:

...Far be it from me that I should sin against You, O Lord, by ceasing to pray for others.[6]
1 Samuel 12:23

PRAYER REQUESTS AND PRAISES
TODAY'S DATE:

My personal request:

Confidential requests from my friends:

*Be joyful always; pray continually; give thanks in all circumstances,
for this is God's will for you in Christ Jesus.
1 Thessalonians 5:16-18 NIV*

PRAYER REQUESTS AND PRAISES
TODAY'S DATE:

My personal request:

Confidential requests from my friends:

*Let us therefore come boldly to the throne of grace,
that we may obtain mercy and find grace to help in time of need.*
Hebrews 4:16

PRAYER REQUESTS AND PRAISES
TODAY'S DATE:

My personal request:

Confidential requests from my friends:

I pray that out of His glorious riches
He may strengthen you with power through His Spirit in your inner being.
Ephesians 3:16 NIV

PRAYER REQUESTS AND PRAISES
TODAY'S DATE:

My personal request:

Confidential requests from my friends:

We can be confident that He will listen to us whenever we ask Him for anything
in line with His will and . . . we can be sure that He will give us what we ask for.
1 John 5:14-15 NLT

PRAYER REQUESTS AND PRAISES
TODAY'S DATE:

My personal request:

Confidential requests from my friends:

Let us come before His presence with thanksgiving:
and let us shout joyfully to Him with psalms.
Psalms 95:2

PRAYER REQUESTS AND PRAISES
TODAY'S DATE:

My personal request:

Confidential requests from my friends:

Then you will call upon Me and come and pray to Me, and I will listen to you.
Jeremiah 29:12 (BOA)

PRAYER REQUESTS AND PRAISES
TODAY'S DATE:

My personal request:

Confidential requests from my friends:

...the Spirit Himself makes intercession for us with groanings which cannot be uttered.
Romans 8:26

PRAYER REQUESTS AND PRAISES
TODAY'S DATE:

My personal request:

Confidential requests from my friends:

Until now you have not asked for anything in My name.
Ask and you will receive, and your joy will be complete.
John 16:24

PRAYER REQUESTS AND PRAISES
TODAY'S DATE:

My personal request:

Confidential requests from my friends:

Then Jesus told His disciples a parable
to show them that they should always pray and not give up.
Luke 18:1

PRAYER REQUESTS AND PRAISES
TODAY'S DATE:

My personal request:

Confidential requests from my friends:

*Then Jesus told His disciples a parable
to show them that they should always pray and not give up.
Luke 18:1*

OTHER STUDIES BY
ELIZABETH BAGWELL FICKEN

And the Lord Blessed Job: An in-depth study of Job

One of the Lord's blessings to Job was that he was chosen to show Satan that God is worthy of worship no matter what happens in our lives. While the book of Job deals with suffering, it isn't about answering the question "why do people suffer?" It's about humbly submitting to God as the Holy One who is infinite in wisdom, power, justice, and goodness.

That You May Know the Lord: An in-depth study of Ezekiel

Don't miss this great book! As you study this intriguing prophecy, you will be humbled by the holiness, sovereignty and glory of God; you will be challenged to examine your own lives as you see the sin of the Israelites; you will be inspired as you see the power of the Holy Spirit; and you will be excited as you anticipate wonderful promises to be fulfilled by the Lord.

Follow Me: An in-depth study of the Gospel of Matthew

This study will challenge you to a more passionate commitment to Jesus. Learn from Matthew's eye-witness perspective, his proofs from Old Testament scriptures, and his presentation of Jesus' five sermons, just who Jesus is, what He did, and what He said. Matthew's life was drastically changed from his encounter with Jesus—yours will be too.

Letters to the Thessalonians: An in-depth study of 1st and 2nd Thessalonians

These letters are about faith, hope and love; holiness, prayer, and perseverance; the will of God and the glorious return of Christ. And so much more! Almost every major doctrine of our faith is covered in these personal writings from the apostle Paul. Join me as we read someone else's mail. I'm sure you'll find a few things that you will think were written just to you!

Come Let Us Worship: An in-depth study of Psalms

The Psalms contain many of our most well-known Scriptures, offering comfort and expressing the emotions of our souls. They challenge us to godly living, always trusting the Lord. What a beautiful arrangement of poems, prayers, and praises God has given us! From Psalm 1 to Psalm 150, you'll study selected psalms in the order of their placement in the Scriptures.

Find her! elizabethficken.com or

Available at
amazon.com
and other bookstores